In the Pines

A Forest of Paper-Pieced Quilts

12 Easy & Accurate Patterns

Carolyn Cullinan McCormick

In the Pines
A Forest of Paper-Pieced Quilts

12 Easy & Accurate Patterns

Text copyright 2015
Carolyn Cullinan McCormick

Publisher: Amy Marson

Creative Director: Gailen Runge

Editors: Donna di Natale and Edie McGinnis

Technical Editor: Jane Miller

Cover/Book Designer: Kim Walsh

Photography: Aaron T. Leimkuehler

Illustration: Eric Sears

Photo Editor: Jo Ann Groves

Published by Kansas City Star Quilts, an imprint of C&T Publishing, Inc., P.O. Box 1456, Lafayette, CA 94549

Attention Teachers: C&T Publishing, Inc., encourages you to use this book as a text for teaching. Contact us at 800-284-1114 or ctpub.com for lesson plans and information about the C&T Creative Troupe.

We take great care to ensure that the information included in our products is accurate and presented in good faith, but no warranty is provided nor are results guaranteed. Having no control over the choices of materials or procedures used, neither the author nor C&T Publishing, Inc., shall have any liability to any person or entity with respect to any loss or damage caused directly or indirectly by the information contained in this book. For your convenience, we post an up-to-date listing of corrections on our website (ctpub.com). If a correction is not already noted, please contact our customer service department at ctinfo@ctpub.com or at P.O. Box 1456, Lafayette, CA 94549.

Trademark (™) and registered trademark (®) names are used throughout this book. Rather than use the symbols with every occurrence of a trademark or registered trademark name, we are using the names only in the editorial fashion and to the benefit of the owner, with no intention of infringement.

ISBN: 978-1-61745-330-4

Library of Congress: 2015953566

*C*arolyn Cullinan McCormick currently lives in Franktown, Colorado, which is just a hop, skip and a jump from Denver, with her husband, Larry. They have a son, Ryan, and a daughter, Jennifer. Ryan and his wife, Megan, have two little girls, McKenna Carolyn and Kate Elizabeth. Jennifer and her husband, Anthony, have a son, Lincoln Larry, and a daughter, Keira Lyn.

Carolyn started to quilt in 1985 when she and her family moved to Bozeman, Montana. There she worked and taught a variety of quilting and craft classes at The Patchworks from 1987 to 1995. In 1995, she invented the Add-A-Quarter ruler to make rotary cutting of templates easier. The Add-A-Quarter has now become a standard tool for paper piecing.

Carolyn has invented other tools as well: The Add-An-Eighth, Add-Three-Eighths and the Add-Enough are more of the gadgets that make life much easier for quilters. You can see all her products and books at addaquarter.com.

Dedication

*T*he tree represents family. If you have a strong base you are able to branch out in many directions. Thanks to my family for letting me branch out!! I am so blessed to have your love and support.

Acknowledgments

*T*hanks to my amazing husband, Larry. You are the love of my life, and I cannot believe that I am so blessed to have you in my life.

A very special thank you to family and friends for testing blocks for me. I understand how busy everyone is, and that makes me appreciate you even more. Tree of Paradise (Romance of Patchwork) made by Megan McCormick, Parker, Colorado; Tree of Life (1938) made by Carol Netwal, Castle Rock, Colorado; Tennessee Pine made by Diane Donnelly, Bozeman, Montana; Tree (Dakota Farmer) made by Carol Bonetti, Castle Rock, Colorado; Tree of Paradise (Bureau Farmer) made by Marilyn Vap, Castle Rock, Colorado; Pine Tree (Nancy Page) made by Bonnie Colonna, Castle Rock, Colorado; Tree of Life (Capper's) made by Jan Korytkowski, Castle Rock, Colorado; Tree of Life (Safford & Bishop) made by Ginny Rafferty, Castle Rock, Colorado; Tree of Paradise made by Connie Stewart, Castle Rock, Colorado; Pine Tree (McKim) made by Nancy Plekan, Parker, Colorado; Christmas Tree made by Wendy Kay, Castle Rock, Colorado; and Pine Tree (Nancy Cabot) made by Marie Llanes, Denver.

I would like to thank Carol Willey, Susan Bateman and Bonnie Colonna for their amazing long-arm quilting. Your talents always make the quilts look wonderful.

Thanks to the staff of Kansas City Star Quilts. No book comes together without a talented team of people working on it. Doug, Edie, Donna, Jane, Eric, Kim, Aaron and Jo Ann; these are some of the people who make Kansas City Star Quilts books so amazing. Thank you.

The following people and companies graciously sent fabric and batting for the quilts: Lissa Alexander with Moda Fabrics, Teresa Coates with Robert Kaufman Fabrics and Lindsey Grand with The Warm Company. Thank you, thank you, thank you!

Introduction

The first pattern The Kansas City Star published in 1928 was called Pine Tree. The pattern was printed with full-size pieces and recommendations on what colors to use. The directions read, "The best way is to trace the patterns on cardboard, mark and cut to complete your pattern. Lay the cardboard patterns on the material. The pattern is drawn with pencil carefully. Cut a seam larger, sewing on the pencil line."

I sincerely admire the women who made tree quilts so many years ago. It required a great deal of dedication on the part of the quilter to cut and stitch so many half-square triangles by hand. And, as anyone who has hand-pieced a quilt knows, marking the stitching lines can only be described as tedious. Thankfully, there is more than one way to make a quilt, and we can do away with all that tedious marking. We don't even have to trace the patterns. Instead we can step up to the nearest copy machine and be off and running in no time at all.

Paper-piecing is the fastest and most accurate process for making tree quilts. All those tiny triangles behave themselves like good little soldiers, and the bias edges of the pieces become insignificant because they have been stabilized.

I hope you enjoy the tree designs I have chosen. Each pattern has the potential to make a striking quilt in its own right. Combine them all into a sampler, and the "wow" factor multiplies.

Happy quilting,

Carolyn

Table of Contents

Fire on the Mountain

Size: 72" x 90" quilted

SUPPLY LIST

Use this supply list to create Fire on the Mountain, or as a guide for making a quilt of your own design.

Fabric Requirements:

12 Blocks (one of each pattern):

Light	3/4 yd of 14 fabrics
Dark	5/8 yd of 13 fabrics
Red Print	5/8 yd
Brown	1/8 yd

Sashing, 2nd Border & Binding (Red)	3 3/8 yd
1st Border (Green)	5/8 yd
3rd Border (Green)	1 1/2 yd
Backing	5 1/2 yd
Batting	2 1/4 yd (90" wide)

Make the Blocks

Follow the instructions for making one of each block pattern.

Follow the Finishing Instructions on pages 52-57.

Tree of Life

1938

10" Block

Patterns: pages 61-64

Cutting Instructions

Note: Some strips may have fabric left over. Measurements were figured on 40" wide fabric.

From the light fabric, cut:
1 – 6" x 12" strip – Cut the strip into 2 – 6" squares. Cut the squares from corner to corner once on the diagonal to make triangles.

3 – 2 1/4" x WOF strips – Cut the strips into 47 – 2 1/4" squares. Cut the squares from corner to corner once on the diagonal to make triangles. (1 will be left over)

From the red fabric, cut:
1 – 3 1/4" x 8 1/4" strip – Cut the strip into 2 – 2 1/2" x 3 1/4" rectangles and 1 – 3 1/4" square. Cut the square from corner to corner once on the diagonal to make triangles. (1 will be left over)

2 – 2 1/4" x WOF strips – Cut the strips into 30 – 2 1/4" squares. Cut the squares from corner to corner once on the diagonal to make triangles. (1 will be left over)

1 – 1 3/4" x 10 1/2" strip – Cut the strip into 6 – 1 3/4" squares.

From the dark fabric, cut:
1 – 3 1/4" x 6 1/2" strip – Cut the strip into 2 – 2 1/2" x 3 1/4" rectangles and 1 – 1 1/2" x 3 1/4" rectangle.

1 – 2 1/2" square – Cut the square from corner to corner once on the diagonal to make triangles.

2 – 2 1/4" x WOF strips – Cut the strips into 26 – 2 1/4" squares. Cut the squares from corner to corner once on the diagonal to make triangles. (1 will be left over)

	Fabric	Position	Size	
Unit A – Make 1				
	Red	1	1 3/4" x 1 3/4"	
	Dark	2,6,10,14	2 1/4" x 2 1/4"	
	Light	3,5,7,9,11,13,15	2 1/4" x 2 1/4"	
	Red	4,8,12,16	2 1/4" x 2 1/4"	
Unit B – Make 1				
	Red	1,5,9,13	2 1/4" x 2 1/4"	
	Light	2,4,6,8,10,12,14,18	2 1/4" x 2 1/4"	
	Dark	3,7,11,15,17	2 1/4" x 2 1/4"	
	Red	16	1 3/4" x 1 3/4"	

Unit C – Make 1				
	Light	1,3,7,9,11,13,15,17,19	2 1/4" x 2 1/4"	◻
	Red	2,8,12,16,20	2 1/4" x 2 1/4"	◻
	Dark	4,6,10,14,18	2 1/4" x 2 1/4"	◻
	Red	5	1 3/4" x 1 3/4"	
Unit D – Make 1				
	Red	1,5,9,13,19	2 1/4" x 2 1/4"	◻
	Light	2,4,6,8,10,12,14,18,20,22	2 1/4" x 2 1/4"	◻
	Dark	3,7,11,15,17,21	2 1/4" x 2 1/4"	◻
	Red	16	1 3/4" x 1 3/4"	
Unit E – Make 1				
	Light	1,3,5,7,11,13,15,17,19,21,23	2 1/4" x 2 1/4"	◻
	Red	2,6,12,16,20,24	2 1/4" x 2 1/4"	◻
	Dark	4,8,10,14,18,22	2 1/4" x 2 1/4"	◻
	Red	9	1 3/4" x 1 3/4"	
Unit F – Make 1				
	Red	1,5	2 1/4" x 2 1/4"	◻
	Light	2,4,6	2 1/4" x 2 1/4"	◻
	Dark	3,7	2 1/4" x 2 1/4"	◻
Unit G – Make 1				
	Red	1,5,9	2 1/4" x 2 1/4"	◻
	Light	2,4,6,8	2 1/4" x 2 1/4"	◻
	Dark	3,7	2 1/4" x 2 1/4"	◻
Unit H – Make 1				
	Red	1,5,9	2 1/4" x 2 1/4"	◻
	Light	2,4,6,8,10	2 1/4" x 2 1/4"	◻
	Dark	3,7,11	2 1/4" x 2 1/4"	◻
Unit I – Make 1				
	Red	1,5,9,13	2 1/4" x 2 1/4"	◻
	Light	2,4,6,8,10,12	2 1/4" x 2 1/4"	◻
	Dark	3,7,11	2 1/4" x 2 1/4"	◻
Unit J – Make 1				
	Red	1,5,9,13	2 1/4" x 2 1/4"	◻
	Light	2,4,6,8,10,12,14	2 1/4" x 2 1/4"	◻
	Dark	3,7,11,15	2 1/4" x 2 1/4"	◻
Unit K – Make 1				
	Red	1	3 1/4" x 3 1/4"	◻
	Dark	2,3	2 1/2" x 2 1/2"	◻
	Dark	4,6	2 1/2" x 3 1/4"	

	Red	5,7	2 1/2" x 3 1/4"
	Dark	8	1 1/2" x 3 1/4"
Unit L – Make 1			
	Red	1	1 3/4" x 1 3/4"
	Light	2,3	2 1/4" x 2 1/4" ◻
Units M & N – Make 1 each			
	Light	1	6" x 6" ◻
	Dark	2	2 1/4" x 2 1/4" ◻
Unit O – Make 1			
	Red	1,3,5,7,9,11,13	2 1/4" x 2 1/4" ◻
	Light	2,4,6,8,10,12	2 1/4" x 2 1/4" ◻
Unit P – Make 1			
	Dark	1,3,5,7,9	2 1/4" x 2 1/4" ◻
	Light	2,4,6,8,10	2 1/4" x 2 1/4" ◻
	Red	11	2 1/4" x 2 1/4" ◻
Unit Q – Make 1			
	Red	1,5,7,9	2 1/4" x 2 1/4" ◻
	Light	2,4,6,8	2 1/4" x 2 1/4" ◻
	Dark	3	2 1/4" x 2 1/4" ◻
Unit R – Make 1			
	Red	1,3,7	2 1/4" x 2 1/4" ◻
	Light	2,4,6	2 1/4" x 2 1/4" ◻
	Dark	5	2 1/4" x 2 1/4" ◻
Unit S – Make 1			
	Red	1,5	2 1/4" x 2 1/4" ◻
	Light	2,4	2 1/4" x 2 1/4" ◻
	Dark	3	2 1/4" x 2 1/4" ◻
Unit T – Make 1			
	Light	1	2 1/4" x 2 1/4" ◻
	Red	2,3	2 1/4" x 2 1/4" ◻
	Dark	4	2 1/4" x 2 1/4" ◻
Units U & V – Make 1 each			
	Light	1	6" x 6" ◻

1. Sew unit B to unit A.

2. Sew unit C to unit AB.

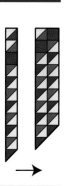

3. Sew unit D to unit ABC.

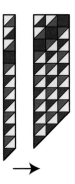

4. Sew unit E to unit ABCD.

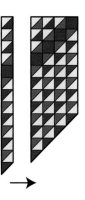

5. Sew unit ABCDE to unit U.

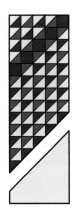

6. Sew unit F to unit G.

7. Sew unit FG to unit H.

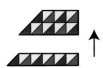

8. Sew unit FGH to unit I.

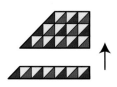

9. Sew unit FGHI to unit J.

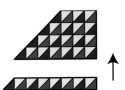

10. Sew unit V to unit FGHIJ.

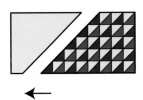

11. Sew units M and N on each side of unit K.

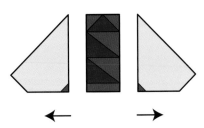

12. Sew unit L to unit MKN.

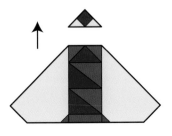

13. Sew unit O to unit P.

14. Sew unit OP to unit Q.

15. Sew unit OPQ to unit R.

16. Sew unit OPQR to unit S.

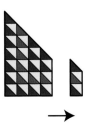

17. Sew unit OPQRS to unit T.

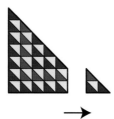

18. Sew together as shown.

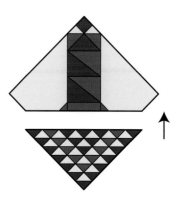

19. Sew together as shown.

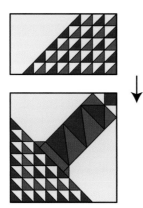

20. Sew together as shown.

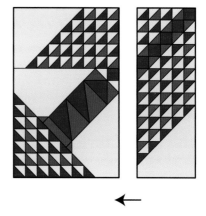

Pine Tree

Nancy Page - January 11, 1934

10" Block

Patterns: pages 65-67

Cutting Instructions

Note: Some strips may have fabric left over. Measurements were figured on 40" wide fabric.

From the light fabric, cut:

1 – 4 1/2" x 13 1/2" strip – Cut the strip into 3 – 4 1/2" squares. Cut **1** square from corner to corner once on the diagonal to make triangles.

2 – 2 1/2" x WOF strips – Cut the strips into 23 – 2 1/2" squares. Cut the squares from corner to corner once on the diagonal to make triangles. (1 piece will be left over)

1 – 2" x 14" strip – Cut the strip into 2 – 2" x 4" rectangles and 3 – 2" squares.

From the dark fabric, cut:

1 – 5 1/2" square – Cut the square from corner to corner once on the diagonal to make triangles.

1 – 3" x 4 1/2" rectangle.

2 – 2 1/2" x WOF strips – Cut the strip into 26 – 2 1/2" squares. Cut the squares from corner to corner once on the diagonal to make triangles. (1 piece will be left over)

	Fabric	Position	Size
Unit A – Make 1			
	Dark	1,3,5,7,9	2 1/2" x 2 1/2" ◩
	Light	2,4,6,8,10	2 1/2" x 2 1/2" ◩
	Light	11	2" x 4"
Unit B – Make 1			
	Dark	1,3,5,7,9,11,13,15	2 1/2" x 2 1/2" ◩
	Light	2,4,6,8,10,12,16	2 1/2" x 2 1/2" ◩
	Light	14	2" x 2"
Unit C – Make 1			
	Light	1,3,7,9,11,13,15,17	2 1/2" x 2 1/2" ◩
	Dark	2,4,6,8,10,12,14,16,18	2 1/2" x 2 1/2" ◩
	Light	5	2" x 2"
Unit D – Make 1			
	Light	1,3,5,7,9,11,15,17,19	2 1/2" x 2 1/2" ◩
	Dark	2,4,6,8,10,12,14,16,18	2 1/2" x 2 1/2" ◩
	Light	13	2" x 2"
Unit E – Make 1			
	Dark	1	2 1/2" x 2 1/2" ◩
	Light	2	2 1/2" x 2 1/2" ◩
	Light	3	2" x 4"
Unit F – Make 1			
	Dark	1,3,5,7,9	2 1/2" x 2 1/2" ◩
	Light	2,4,6,8	2 1/2" x 2 1/2" ◩
Unit G – Make 1			
	Dark	1,3,5,7,9,11	2 1/2" x 2 1/2" ◩
	Light	2,4,6,8,10	2 1/2" x 2 1/2" ◩
Unit H – Make 1			
	Light	1,3,5,7,9,11	2 1/2" x 2 1/2" ◩
	Dark	2,4,6,8,10,12	2 1/2" x 2 1/2" ◩
Unit I – Make 1			
	Light	1	4 1/2" x 4 1/2"
	Dark	2	2 1/2" x 2 1/2" ◩
	Dark	3	3" x 4 1/2"
Unit J – Make 1			
	Light	1	4 1/2" x 4 1/2"
	Dark	2	2 1/2" x 2 1/2" ◩
Units K & L – Make 1 each			
	Dark	1	5 1/2" x 5 1/2" ◩
Units M & N – Make 1 each			
	Light	1	4 1/2" x 4 1/2" ◩

To Make the Block

1. Sew unit B to unit A.

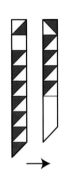

2. Sew unit C to unit AB.

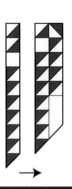

3. Sew unit D to unit ABC.

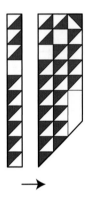

4. Sew unit E to unit F.

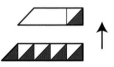

5. Sew unit G to unit EF.

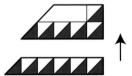

6. Sew unit H to unit EFG.

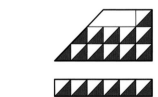

7. Sew unit J to unit I.

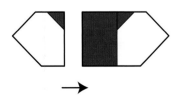

8. Sew unit K to unit IJ.

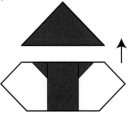

9. Sew unit L to unit IJK.

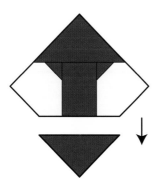

10. Sew together as shown.

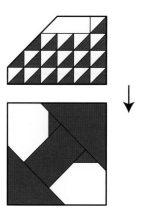

11. Sew together as shown.

12. Sew units N and M to each side of block.

Tree-of-Paradise

The Romance of the Patchwork Quilt in America, Carrie Hall 1935

10" Block

Patterns: pages 68-70

Cutting Instructions

Note: Some strips may have fabric left over. Measurements were figured on 40" wide fabric.

From the light fabric, cut:

1 – 5 3/4" square – Cut the square from corner to corner once on the diagonal to make triangles.

1 – 4 1/2" x 10" strip – Cut the strip into 2 – 4 1/2" x 5" rectangles.

1 – 3" x WOF strip – Cut the strip into 9 – 3" squares. Cut the squares from corner to corner once on the diagonal to make triangles.

From the medium fabric, cut:

1 – 4 1/2" square – Cut the squares from corner to corner once on the diagonal to make triangles.

1 – 3" x 18" strip – Cut the strip into 6 – 3" squares. Cut the squares from corner to corner once on the diagonal to make triangles.

1 – 2 1/2" x 18 3/4" strip – Cut the strip into 3 – 2 1/2" squares, 1 – 2 1/2" x 5 1/4" rectangle and 2 – 2 1/2" x 3" rectangles.

From the dark fabric, cut:

1 – 3" x WOF strip – Cut the strip into 6 – 3" squares. Cut the squares from corner to corner once on the diagonal to make triangles.

	Fabric	Position	Size	
Unit A – Make 1				
	Medium	1	2 1/2" x 2 1/2"	
	Dark	2,6	3" x 3"	◲
	Light	3,5,7	3" x 3"	◲
	Medium	4,8	3" x 3"	◲
Unit B – Make 1				
	Medium	1,5	3" x 3"	◲
	Dark	3,7,9	3" x 3"	◲
	Medium	8	2 1/2" x 2 1/2"	
	Light	2,4,6,10	3" x 3"	◲
Unit C – Make 1				
	Light	1,3,7,9,11	3" x 3"	◲
	Medium	2,8,12	3" x 3"	◲
	Dark	4,6,10	3" x 3"	◲
	Medium	5	2 1/2" x 2 1/2"	
Unit D – Make 1				
	Dark	1	3" x 3"	◲
	Light	2	3" x 3"	◲
	Medium	3	3" x 3"	◲
Unit E – Make 1				
	Medium	1,5	3" x 3"	◲
	Light	2,4	3" x 3"	◲
	Dark	3	3" x 3"	◲
Unit F – Make 1				
	Dark	1,5	3" x 3"	◲
	Light	2,4,6	3" x 3"	◲
	Medium	3,7	3" x 3"	◲
Unit G – Make 1				
	Light	1	4 1/2" x 5"	
	Medium	2	2 1/2" x 3"	
	Medium	3	2 1/2" x 5 1/4"	
Unit H – Make 1				
	Light	1	4 1/2" x 5"	
	Medium	2	2 1/2" x 3"	
Units I & J – Make 1 each				
	Medium	1	4 1/2" x 4 1/2"	◲
Units K & L – Make 1 each				
	Light	1	5 3/4" x 5 3/4"	◲

To Make the Block

---

1. Sew unit B to unit A.

2. Sew unit C to unit AB.

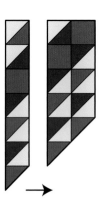

---

3. Sew unit D to unit E.

4. Sew unit F to unit DE.

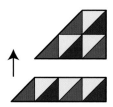

---

5. Sew unit H to unit G.

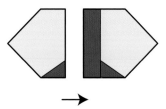

---

6. Sew units I and J to unit GH.

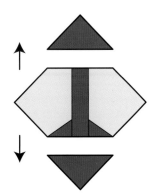

7. Sew together as shown.

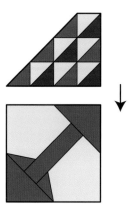

8. Sew together as shown.

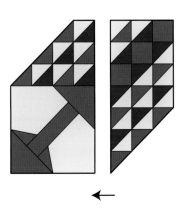

9. Sew units K and L to each side of block.

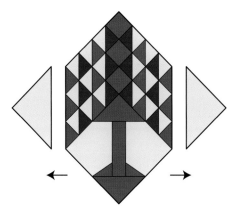

Tree of Paradise

10" Block

Patterns: pages 71-73

Cutting Instructions

Note: Some strips may have fabric left over. Measurements were figured on 40" wide fabric.

From the light fabric, cut:

1 – 5 1/2" square – Cut the square from corner to corner once on the diagonal to make triangles.

1 – 4 1/2" x 13 1/2" strip – Cut the strip into 3 – 4 1/2" squares. Cut **1** square from corner to corner once on the diagonal to make triangles. (1 piece will be left over)

2 – 2 1/2" strips x WOF strips – Cut the strips into 20 – 2 1/2" squares. Cut the squares from corner to corner once on the diagonal to make triangles.

1 – 2" x 8" strip – Cut the strip into 4 – 2" squares.

From the dark fabric, cut:

1 – 5 1/2" square – Cut the square from corner to corner once on the diagonal to make triangles.
(One piece will be left over)

1 – 3" x 4 1/2" rectangle.

2 – 2 1/2" x WOF strip – Cut the strip into 25 – 2 1/2" squares. Cut the squares from corner to corner once on the diagonal to make triangles.

	Fabric	Position	Size	
Unit A – Make 1				
	Light	1	2" x 2"	
	Dark	2,4,6,8,10,12	2 1/2" x 2 1/2"	◻
	Light	3,5,7,9,11	2 1/2" x 2 1/2"	◻
Unit B – Make 1				
	Dark	1,3,5,7,9,11,13	2 1/2" x 2 1/2"	◻
	Light	2,4,6,8,10,14	2 1/2" x 2 1/2"	◻
	Light	12	2" x 2"	
Unit C – Make 1				
	Light	1,3,7,9,11,13,15	2 1/2" x 2 1/2"	◻
	Dark	2,4,6,8,10,12,14,16	2 1/2" x 2 1/2"	◻
	Light	5	2" x 2"	
Unit D – Make 1				
	Dark	1,3,5,7,9,11,13,15,17	2 1/2" x 2 1/2"	◻
	Light	2,4,6,8,10,14,16,18	2 1/2" x 2 1/2"	◻
	Light	12	2" x 2"	
Unit E – Make 1				
	Dark	1,3,5	2 1/2" x 2 1/2"	◻
	Light	2,4	2 1/2" x 2 1/2"	◻
Unit F – Make 1				
	Dark	1,3,5,7	2 1/2" x 2 1/2"	◻
	Light	2,4,6	2 1/2" x 2 1/2"	◻
Unit G – Make 1				
	Dark	1,3,5,7,9	2 1/2" x 2 1/2"	◻
	Light	2,4,6,8	2 1/2" x 2 1/2"	◻
Unit H – Make 1				
	Dark	1,3,5,7,9,11	2 1/2" x 2 1/2"	◻
	Light	2,4,6,8,10	2 1/2" x 2 1/2"	◻
Units I & J – Make 1 each				
	Light	1	5 1/2" x 5 1/2"	◻
Unit K – Make 1				
	Light	1	4 1/2" x 4 1/2"	
	Dark	2	2 1/2" x 2 1/2"	◻
	Dark	3	3" x 4 1/2"	
Unit L – Make 1				
	Light	1	4 1/2" x 4 1/2"	
	Dark	2	2 1/2" x 2 1/2"	◻
Unit M – Make 1				
	Dark	1	5 1/2" x 5 1/2"	◻
Unit N – Make 1				
	Light	1	4 1/2" x 4 1/2"	◻

To Make the Block

1. Sew unit B to unit A.

2. Sew unit C to unit AB.

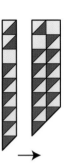

3. Sew unit D to unit ABC.

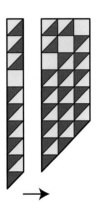

4. Sew unit E to unit F.

5. Sew unit EF to unit G.

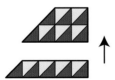

6. Sew unit H to unit EFG.

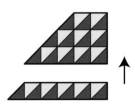

7. Sew unit L to unit K.

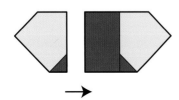

8. Sew unit M to unit KL.

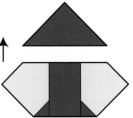

9. Sew unit N to unit KLM.

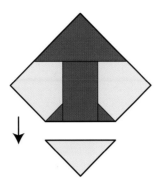

10. Sew together as shown.

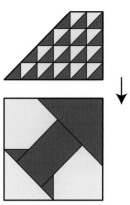

11. Sew together as shown.

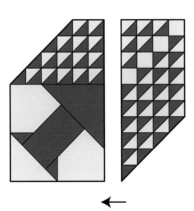

12. Sew units I and J to either side of the block.

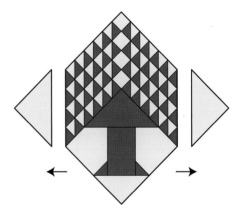

Tree

Dakota Farmer November 15, 1927

10" Block

Patterns: pages 74-76

Cutting Instructions

Note: Some strips may have fabric left over. Measurements were figured on 40" wide fabric.

From the light fabric, cut:
1 – 5 1/2" x 20 1/2" strip – Cut the strip into 2 – 4 3/4" x 5 1/2" rectangles and 2 – 5 1/2" squares. Cut the squares from corner to corner once on the diagonal to make triangles. (1 piece will be left over)

1 – 2 1/2" x WOF strip – Cut the strip into 15 – 2 1/2" squares. Cut the squares from corner to corner once on the diagonal to make triangles.

1 – 2" x 6" strip – Cut the strip into 3 – 2" squares.

From the dark fabric, cut:
1 – 5 1/2" x 8" strip. Cut the strip into 1 – 2 1/2" x 5 1/2" rectangle and 1 – 5 1/2" square. Cut the square from corner to corner once on the diagonal to make triangles. (1 piece will be left over)

2 – 2 1/2" x WOF strips – Cut the strips into 19 – 2 1/2" squares. Cut the squares from corner to corner once on the diagonal to make triangles.

	Fabric	Position	Size
Unit A – Make 1			
	Light	1	2" x 2"
	Dark	2,4,6,8,10,12	2 1/2" x 2 1/2" ◻
	Light	3,5,7,9,11	2 1/2" x 2 1/2" ◻
Unit B – Make 1			
	Dark	1,3,5,7,9,11,13	2 1/2" x 2 1/2" ◻
	Light	2,4,6,8,10,14	2 1/2" x 2 1/2" ◻
	Light	12	2" x 2"
Unit C – Make 1			
	Light	1,3,7,9,11,13,15	2 1/2" x 2 1/2" ◻
	Dark	2,4,6,8,10,12,14,16	2 1/2" x 2 1/2" ◻
	Light	5	2" x 2"
Unit D – Make 1			
	Dark	1,3,5,7	2 1/2" x 2 1/2" ◻
	Light	2,4,6	2 1/2" x 2 1/2" ◻
Unit E – Make 1			
	Dark	1,3,5,7,9	2 1/2" x 2 1/2" ◻
	Light	2,4,6,8	2 1/2" x 2 1/2" ◻
Unit F – Make 1			
	Dark	1,3,5,7,9,11	2 1/2" x 2 1/2" ◻
	Light	2,4,6,8,10	2 1/2" x 2 1/2" ◻
Unit G – Make 1			
	Light	1	4 3/4" x 5 1/2"
	Dark	2	2 1/2" x 2 1/2" ◻
	Dark	3	2 1/2" x 5 1/2"
Unit H – Make 1			
	Light	1	4 3/4" x 5 1/2"
	Dark	2	2 1/2" x 2 1/2" ◻
Unit I – Make 1			
	Dark	1	5 1/2" x 5 1/2" ◻
Units J, K & L – Make 1 each			
	Light	1	5 1/2" x 5 1/2" ◻

To Make the Block

1. Sew unit B to unit A.

2. Sew unit C to unit AB.

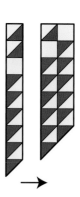

3. Sew unit D to unit E.

4. Sew unit F to unit DE.

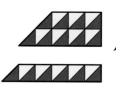

5. Sew unit H to unit G.

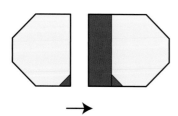

6. Sew unit I to unit GH.

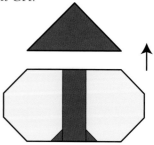

7. Sew unit GHI to unit J.

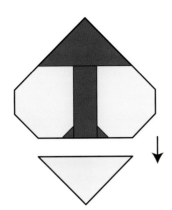

8. Sew together as shown.

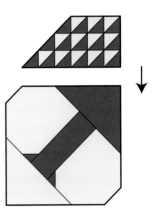

9. Sew together as shown.

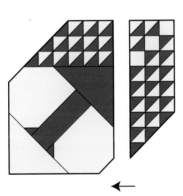

10. Sew units K and L to each side of block.

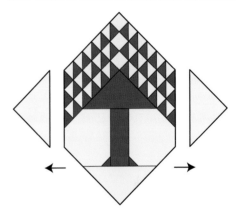

Tree of Paradise

Bureau Farmer - January 1931

10" Block

Patterns: pages 77-79

Cutting Instructions

Note: Some strips may have fabric left over. Measurements were figured on 40" wide fabric.

From the 1st light (lightest) fabric, cut:
1 – 6 1/2" square – Cut the square from corner to corner once on the diagonal to make triangles. (1 piece will be left over)

1 – 3" square

1 – 2 1/2" x WOF strip – Cut the strip into 14 – 2 1/2" squares. Cut the squares from corner to corner once on the diagonal to make triangles.

1 – 2" x 4" strip – Cut the strip into 2 – 2" squares.

From the 2nd light (medium light) fabric, cut:
1 – 6 1/2" square – Cut the square from corner to corner once on the diagonal to make triangles. (1 piece will be left over)

1 – 3" square

1 – 2 1/2" x WOF strip – Cut the strip into 14 – 2 1/2" squares. Cut the squares from corner to corner once on the diagonal to make triangles.

1 – 2" x 4" strip – Cut the strip into 2 – 2" squares.

From the 1st dark (darkest) fabric, cut:
1 – 2 1/2" x WOF strip – Cut the strip into 12 – 2 1/2" squares. Cut the squares from corner to corner once on the diagonal to make triangles.

From the 2nd dark (medium dark) fabric, cut:
1 – 2 1/2" x WOF strip – Cut the strip into 12 – 2 1/2" squares. Cut the squares from corner to corner once on the diagonal to make triangles.

From the brown fabric, cut:
1 – 4 1/2" square – Cut the square from corner to corner once on the diagonal to make triangles.

1 – 2 1/2" x 5 1/2" rectangle.

	Fabric	Position	Size	
Unit A – Make 1				
	Light/Light	1	2 1/2" x 2 1/2"	◩
	Medium/Light	2,4,6,8,10,12,14,16,18,20	2 1/2" x 2 1/2"	◩
	Dark/Dark	3,5,7,9,11,13,15,17,19	2 1/2" x 2 1/2"	◩
Unit B – Make 1				
	Medium/Light	1	2" x 2"	
	Medium/Light	2,4,6,8,10,12,14,16	2 1/2" x 2 1/2"	◩
	Dark/Dark	3,5,7,9,11,13,15	2 1/2" x 2 1/2"	◩
	Light/Light	17,19	2 1/2" x 2 1/2"	◩
	Medium/Dark	18	2 1/2" x 2 1/2"	◩
Unit C – Make 1				
	Light/Light	1,3,5	2 1/2" x 2 1/2"	◩
	Medium/Light	6,8,10,12,14,16	2 1/2" x 2 1/2"	◩
	Medium/Dark	2,4	2 1/2" x 2 1/2"	◩
	Dark/Dark	7,9,11,13,15	2 1/2" x 2 1/2"	◩
Unit D – Make 1				
	Medium/Light	1	2" x 2"	
	Medium/Light	2,4,6,8	2 1/2" x 2 1/2"	◩
	Dark/Dark	3,5,7	2 1/2" x 2 1/2"	◩
	Light/Light	9,11,13,15	2 1/2" x 2 1/2"	◩
	Medium/Dark	10,12,14	2 1/2" x 2 1/2"	◩
Unit E – Make 1				
	Medium/Dark	1,3,5,7,9,11	2 1/2" x 2 1/2"	◩
	Light/Light	2,4,6,8,10,12	2 1/2" x 2 1/2"	◩
Unit F – Make 1				
	Light/Light	1	2" x 2"	
	Light/Light	2,4,6,8,10	2 1/2" x 2 1/2"	◩
	Medium/Dark	3,5,7,9,11	2 1/2" x 2 1/2"	◩
Unit G – Make 1				
	Medium/Dark	1,3,5,7	2 1/2" x 2 1/2"	◩
	Light/Light	2,4,6,8	2 1/2" x 2 1/2"	◩
Unit H – Make 1				
	Light/Light	1	2" x 2"	
	Light/Light	2,4,6	2 1/2" x 2 1/2"	◩
	Medium/Dark	3,5,7	2 1/2" x 2 1/2"	◩
Unit I – Make 1				
	Light/Light	1	3" x 3"	
Unit J – Make 1				
	Medium/Light	1	3" x 3"	
Unit K – Make 1				
	Brown	1	2 1/2" x 5 1/2"	
	Light/Light	2	6 1/2" x 6 1/2"	◩
	Medium/Light	3	6 1/2" x 6 1/2"	◩
	Brown	4,5	4 1/2" x 4 1/2"	◩

To Make the Block

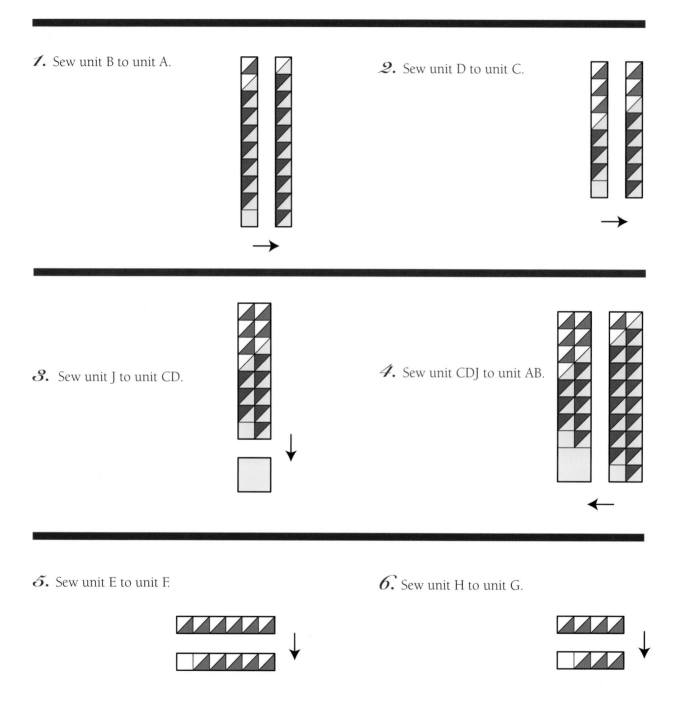

1. Sew unit B to unit A.

2. Sew unit D to unit C.

3. Sew unit J to unit CD.

4. Sew unit CDJ to unit AB.

5. Sew unit E to unit F.

6. Sew unit H to unit G.

7. Sew unit I to unit GH.

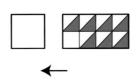

8. Sew unit EF to unit GHI.

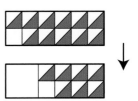

9. Sew unit EFGHI to unit K.

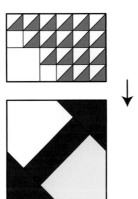

10. Sew together as shown.

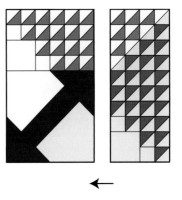

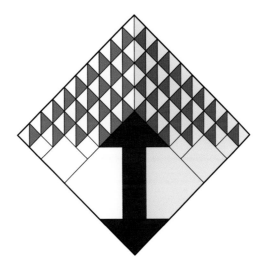

Tennessee Pine

10" Block

Patterns: pages 80-82

Cutting Instructions

Note: Some strips may have fabric left over. Measurements were figured on 40" wide fabric.

From the light fabric, cut:

1 – 5 1/4" square – Cut the square from corner to corner once on the diagonal to make triangles.

1 – 4" square – Cut the square from corner to corner once on the diagonal to make triangles.

1 – 3 1/4" x WOF strip – Cut the strip into 8 – 3 1/4" squares. Cut each square from corner to corner once on the diagonal to make triangles.

1 – 1 3/4" x 14 1/2" strip – Cut the strip into 2 – 1 3/4" x 7 1/4" rectangles.

From the dark fabric, cut:

1 – 4" x 8" strip – Cut the strip into 2 – 4" squares. Cut each square from corner to corner once on the diagonal to make triangles.

1 – 3 1/4" x WOF strip – Cut the strip into 7 – 3 1/4" squares. Cut each square from corner to corner once on the diagonal to make triangles.

1 – 2 3/4" x 8 1/4" rectangle.

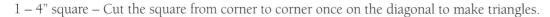

	Fabric	Position	Size	
Units A & C – Make 1 each				
	Dark	1,3,5	3 1/4" x 3 1/4"	◻
	Light	2,4	3 1/4" x 3 1/4"	◻
	Light	6	4" x 4"	◻
Units B & D – Make 1 each				
	Dark	1,3,5,7	3 1/4" x 3 1/4"	◻
	Light	2,4,6	3 1/4" x 3 1/4"	◻
Units E & F – Make 1 each				
	Light	1	5 1/4" x 5 1/4"	◻
Unit G – Make 1				
	Dark	1,4,7,10	4" x 4"	◻
	Light	2,3,5,6,8,9	3 1/4" x 3 1/4"	◻
Unit H – Make 1				
	Dark	1	2 3/4" x 8 1/4"	
	Light	2,3	1 3/4" x 7 1/4"	

To Make the Block

1. Sew unit A to unit B.

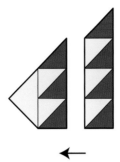

2. Sew unit E to unit AB.

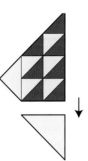

3. Sew unit D to unit C.

4. Sew unit F to unit CD.

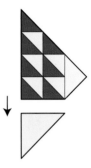

5. Sew unit G to unit H.

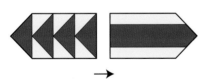

6. Sew together as shown.

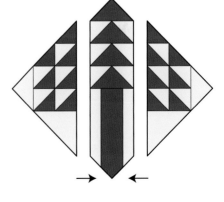

Tree of Life

Capper's Weekly

10" Block

Patterns: pages 83-85

Cutting Instructions

Note: Some strips may have fabric left over. Measurements were figured on 40" wide fabric.

From the light fabric, cut:

1 – 6 3/4" square – Cut the square once on the diagonal to make triangles.

1 – 4 1/4" square – Cut the square from corner to corner once on the diagonal to make triangles. (1 piece will be left)

2 – 2 1/2" x WOF strips – Cut the strips into 21 – 2 1/2" squares. Cut the squares once on the diagonal to make triangles.

1 – 2" x 6" strip – Cut the strip into 3 – 2" squares.

From the red fabric, cut:

1 – 8" square – Cut the square once on the diagonal to make triangles. (1 piece will be left over)

1 – 4 1/4" square – Cut the square once on the diagonal to make triangles.

1 – 2 3/4" square – Cut the square once on the diagonal to make triangles.

1 – 2 1/4" x 5" rectangle.

From the dark fabric, cut:

2 – 2 1/2" x WOF strips – Cut the strips into 24 – 2 1/2" squares. Cut the squares once on the diagonal to make triangles.

	Fabric	Position	Size	
Unit A – Make 1				
	Light	1	2" x 2"	
	Dark	2,4,6,8,10,12,14,16	2 1/2" x 2 1/2"	◲
	Light	3,5,7,9,11,13,15	2 1/2" x 2 1/2"	◲
Unit B – Make 1				
	Dark	1,3,5,7,9,11,13,15,17	2 1/2" x 2 1/2"	◲
	Light	2,4,6,8,10,12,14,18	2 1/2" x 2 1/2"	◲
	Light	16	2" x 2"	
Unit C – Make 1				
	Light	1,3,7,9,11,13,15,17,19	2 1/2" x 2 1/2"	◲
	Dark	2,4,6,8,10,12,14,16,18,20	2 1/2" x 2 1/2"	◲
	Light	5	2" x 2"	
Unit D – Make 1				
	Dark	1,3,5,7,9,11	2 1/2" x 2 1/2"	◲
	Light	2,4,6,8,10	2 1/2" x 2 1/2"	◲
Unit E – Make 1				
	Dark	1,3,5,7,9,11,13	2 1/2" x 2 1/2"	◲
	Light	2,4,6,8,10,12	2 1/2" x 2 1/2"	◲
Unit F – Make 1				
	Dark	1,3,5,7,9,11,13,15	2 1/2" x 2 1/2"	◲
	Light	2,4,6,8,10,12,14	2 1/2" x 2 1/2"	◲
Unit G – Make 1				
	Light	1	6 3/4" x 6 3/4"	◲
	Red	2	2 3/4" x 2 3/4"	◲
	Red	3	2 1/4" x 5"	
Unit H – Make 1				
	Light	1	6 3/4" x 6 3/4"	◲
	Red	2	2 3/4" x 2 3/4"	◲
Unit I – Make 1				
	Red	1	8" x 8"	◲
Unit J – Make 1				
	Light	1	4 1/4" x 4 1/4"	◲
Units K & L – Make 1	Red	1	4 1/4" x 4 1/4"	◲

To Make the Block

1. Sew unit B to unit A.

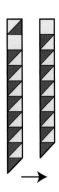

2. Sew unit C to unit AB.

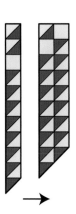

3. Sew unit D to unit E.

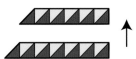

4. Sew unit F to unit DE.

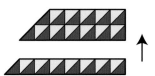

5. Sew unit G to unit H.

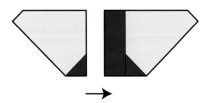

6. Sew unit I to unit GH.

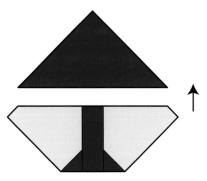

7. Sew unit J to unit GHI.

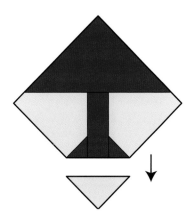

8. Sew together as shown.

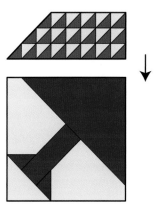

9. Sew together as shown.

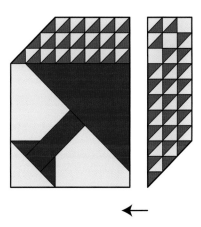

10. Sew units K and L to each side of block.

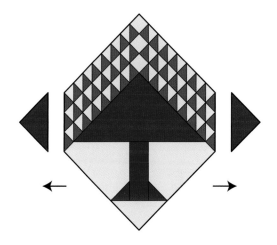

Christmas Tree

Patchwork Quilting in America

10" Block

Patterns: pages 86-88

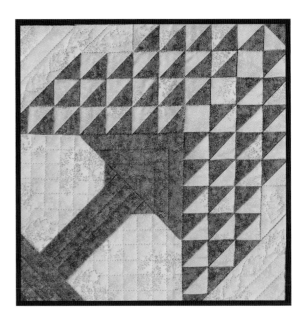

Cutting Instructions

Note: Some strips may have fabric left over. Measurements were figured on 40" wide fabric.

From the light fabric, cut:

1 – 5 1/4" x 15 3/4" strip – Cut the strip into 3 – 5 1/4" squares. Cut **1** square from corner to corner once on the diagonal to make triangles.

2 – 2 1/2" x WOF strips – Cut the strips into 24 – 2 1/2" squares. Cut the squares from corner to corner once on the diagonal to make triangles. 1 piece will be left over.

1 – 2" x 11 1/2" strip – Cut the strip into 3 – 2" squares and 2 – 2" x 2 3/4" rectangles.

From the dark fabric, cut:

1 – 5 1/4" square – Cut the square from corner to corner once on the diagonal to make triangles.

2 – 2 1/2" x WOF strips – Cut the strips into 27 – 2 1/2" squares. Cut the squares from corner to corner once on the diagonal to make triangles. 1 piece will be left over.

1 – 2 1/4" x 5" rectangle.

1 – 2" square – Cut the square from corner to corner once on the diagonal to make triangles.

	Fabric	Position	Size
Unit A – Make 1			
	Dark	1,3,5,7,9,11	2 1/2" x 2 1/2" ◻
	Light	2,4,6,8,10,12	2 1/2" x 2 1/2" ◻
	Light	13	2" x 2 3/4"
Unit B – Make 1			
	Dark	1,3,5,7,9,11,13,15	2 1/2" x 2 1/2" ◻
	Light	2,4,6,8,10,12,16	2 1/2" x 2 1/2" ◻
	Light	14	2" x 2"
Unit C – Make 1			
	Light	1,3,7,9,11,13,15,17	2 1/2" x 2 1/2" ◻
	Dark	2,4,6,8,10,12,14,16,18	2 1/2" x 2 1/2" ◻
	Light	5	2" x 2"
Unit D – Make 1			
	Dark	1,3,5,7,9,11,13,15,17,19	2 1/2" x 2 1/2" ◻
	Light	2,4,6,8,10,12,16,18,20	2 1/2" x 2 1/2" ◻
	Light	14	2" x 2"
Unit E – Make 1			
	Light	1	2" x 2 3/4"
	Light	2,4	2 1/2" x 2 1/2" ◻
	Dark	3,5	2 1/2" x 2 1/2" ◻
Unit F – Make 1			
	Dark	1,3,5,7,9	2 1/2" x 2 1/2" ◻
	Light	2,4,6,8	2 1/2" x 2 1/2" ◻
Unit G – Make 1			
	Dark	1,3,5,7,9,11	2 1/2" x 2 1/2" ◻
	Light	2,4,6,8,10	2 1/2" x 2 1/2" ◻
Unit H – Make 1			
	Dark	1,3,5,7,9,11,13	2 1/2" x 2 1/2" ◻
	Light	2,4,6,8,10,12	2 1/2" x 2 1/2" ◻
Unit I – Make 1			
	Light	1	5 1/4" x 5 1/4"
	Dark	2	2" x 2" ◻
	Dark	3	2 1/4" x 5"
Unit J – Make 1			
	Light	1	5 1/4" x 5 1/4"
	Dark	2	2" x 2" ◻
Units K & L – Make 1 each			
	Light	1	5 1/4" x 5 1/4" ◻
Units M & N – Make 1 each			
	Dark	1	5 1/4" x 5 1/4" ◻

To Make the Block

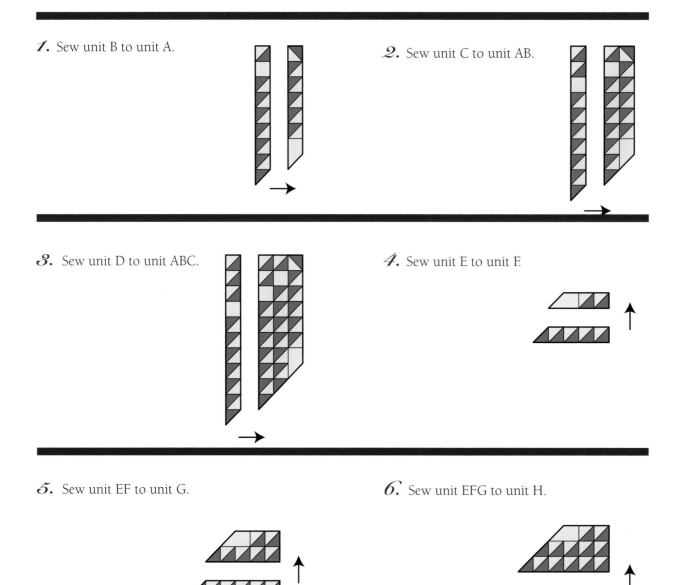

1. Sew unit B to unit A.

2. Sew unit C to unit AB.

3. Sew unit D to unit ABC.

4. Sew unit E to unit F.

5. Sew unit EF to unit G.

6. Sew unit EFG to unit H.

7. Sew unit J to unit I.

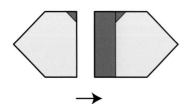

8. Sew units M and N to unit IJ.

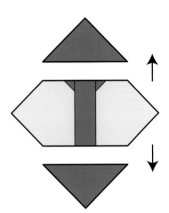

9. Sew together as shown.

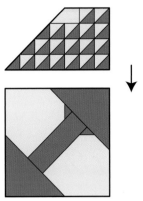

10. Sew together as shown.

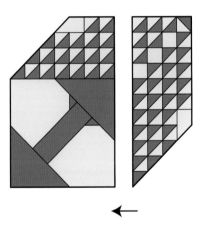

11. Sew units K and L to each side as shown.

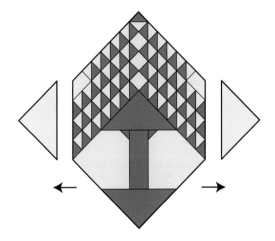

Tree of Life
Safford & Bishop

10" Block

Patterns: pages 89-91

Cutting Instructions

Note: Some strips may have fabric left over. Measurements were figured on 40" wide fabric.

From the light fabric, cut:
1 – 3 3/4" x 7 1/2" strip – Cut the strip into 2 – 3 3/4" squares.

1 – 3 1/2" x 9" strip – Cut the strip into 2 – 3 1/2" x 4 1/2" rectangles.

1 – 2 3/4" x WOF strip – Cut the strip into 14 – 2 3/4" squares. Cut the squares from corner to corner once on the diagonal to make triangles.

1 – 2 1/4" x 14" strip – Cut the strip into 2 – 2 1/4" x 4 3/4" rectangles and 2 – 2 1/4" squares.

From the dark fabric, cut:
1 – 4" square – Cut the square from corner to corner once on the diagonal to make triangles.

1 – 2 3/4" x WOF strip – Cut the strip into 14 – 2 3/4" squares. Cut the squares from corner to corner once on the diagonal to make triangles.

1 – 2 1/4" x 9" strip – Cut the strip into 4 – 2 1/4" squares.

1 – 1 3/4" x 4 1/2" rectangle.

From the red fabric, cut:
1 – 3" square – Cut the square from corner to corner once on the diagonal to make triangles.

	Fabric	Position	Size	
Units A & B – Make 1 each				
	Light	1,3,5	2 3/4" x 2 3/4"	◹
	Dark	2,4,6	2 3/4" x 2 3/4"	◹
	Light	7	2 1/4" x 4 3/4"	
	Light	8	3 3/4" x 3 3/4"	
Unit C – Make 1				
	Dark	1	2 1/4" x 2 1/4"	
	Light	2,4	2 3/4" x 2 3/4"	◹
	Dark	3,5	2 3/4" x 2 3/4"	◹
Unit D – Make 1				
	Dark	1,5	2 3/4" x 2 3/4"	◹
	Light	2,4	2 3/4" x 2 3/4"	◹
	Dark	3	2 1/4" x 2 1/4"	
Unit E – Make 1				
	Dark	1,3,7,9,11,13	2 3/4" x 2 3/4"	◹
	Light	2,4,6,8,10,12	2 3/4" x 2 3/4"	◹
	Dark	5	2 1/4" x 2 1/4"	
	Light	14	2 1/4" x 2 1/4"	
Unit F – Make 1				
	Dark	1,3,5,7,11	2 3/4" x 2 3/4"	◹
	Light	2,4,6,8,10	2 3/4" x 2 3/4"	◹
	Dark	9	2 1/4” x 2 1/4”	
Unit G – Make 1				
	Light	1	2 1/4” x 2 1/4”	
	Dark	2,4,6	2 3/4” x 2 3/4”	◹
	Light	3,5,7	2 3/4” x 2 3/4”	◹
Unit H – Make 1				
	Light	1,3,5,7	2 3/4" x 2 3/4"	◹
	Dark	2,4,6,8	2 3/4" x 2 3/4"	◹
Unit I – Make 1				
	Light	1	3 1/2" x 4 1/2"	
	Red	2	3" x 3"	◹
	Dark	3	1 3/4" x 4 1/2”	
Unit J – Make 1				
	Light	1	3 1/2” x 4 1/2”	
	Red	2	3" x 3"	◹
Units K & L – Make 1 each				
	Dark	1	4” x 4”	◹

To Make the Block

1. Sew unit D to unit C.

2. Sew unit A to unit CD.

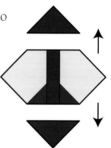

3. Sew unit E to unit ACD.

4. Sew unit G to unit H.

5. Sew unit J to unit I.

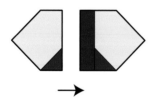

6. Sew units K and L to unit IJ.

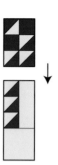

7. Sew unit GH to unit IJKL.

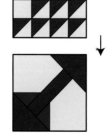

8. Sew unit F to block as shown.

←

9. Sew unit B to block as shown.

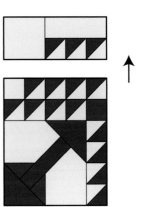

↑

10. Sew together as shown.

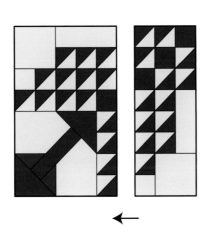

←

Pine Tree

Nancy Cabot

10" Block

Patterns: pages 92-94

Cutting Instructions

Note: Some strips may have fabric left over. Measurements were figured on 40" wide fabric.

From the light fabric, cut:

1 – 4 3/4" x 16 1/4" strip – Cut the strip into 2 – 4 3/4" x 5 3/4" rectangles and 1 – 4 3/4" square. Cut the square from corner to corner once on the diagonal to make triangles.

1 – 2 3/4" x WOF strip – Cut the strip into 13 – 2 3/4" squares. Cut the squares from corner to corner once on the diagonal to make triangles.

1 – 2" x 6" strip – Cut the strip into 3 – 2" squares.

From the dark fabric, cut:

1 – 4 3/4" square – Cut the square from corner to corner once on the diagonal to make triangles.

1 – 3 3/4" x 7 1/2" strip – Cut the strip into 2 – 3 3/4" squares. Cut the squares from corner to corner once on the diagonal to make triangles.

1 – 2 3/4" x WOF strip – Cut the strip into 1 - 2 3/4" x 5 3/4" rectangle and 12 – 2 3/4" squares. Cut the squares from corner to corner once on the diagonal to make triangles.

	Fabric	Position	Size	
Unit A – Make 1				
	Light	1	2" x 2"	
	Dark	2,4,6,8,10,12	2 3/4" x 2 3/4"	◪
	Light	3,5,7,9,11	2 3/4" x 2 3/4"	◪
Units B & J – Make 1 each				
	Dark	1,3	2 3/4" x 2 3/4"	◪
	Light	2,4	2 3/4" x 2 3/4"	◪
Units C & I – Make 1 each				
	Light	1,3	2 3/4" x 2 3/4"	◪
	Dark	2,4	2 3/4" x 2 3/4"	◪
Units D & H – Make 1 each				
	Dark	1	2 3/4" x 2 3/4"	◪
	Light	2,3,4	2 3/4" x 2 3/4"	◪
	Dark	5,6	3 3/4" x 3 3/4"	◪
Unit E – Make 1				
	Dark	1,3,5,7,9,11	2 3/4" x 2 3/4"	◪
	Light	2,4,6,8,10	2 3/4" x 2 3/4"	◪
Units F & G – Make 1 each				
	Light	1	2" x 2"	
	Dark	2	2 3/4" x 2 3/4"	◪
	Light	3	2 3/4" x 2 3/4"	◪
Unit K – Make 1				
	Dark	1	2 3/4" x 5 3/4"	
	Light	2,3	4 3/4" x 5 3/4"	
	Dark	4,5	4 3/4" x 4 3/4"	◪
Units L & M – Make 1 each				
	Light	1	4 3/4" x 4 3/4"	◪

To Make the Block

---

1. Sew unit B to unit C.

2. Sew unit D to unit BC.

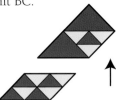

---

3. Sew unit I to unit J.

4. Sew unit IJ to unit H.

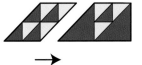

---

5. Sew unit F to unit G.

6. Sew unit K to unit BCD.

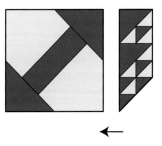

---

7. Sew unit HIJ to Unit FG.

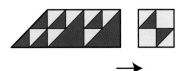

8. Sew unit E to block as shown.

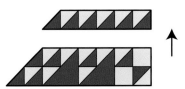

9. Sew together as shown.

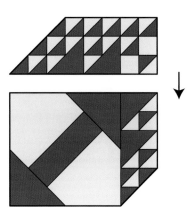

10. Sew unit A to block as shown.

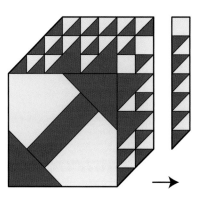

11. Sew units L and M
onto each side of block.

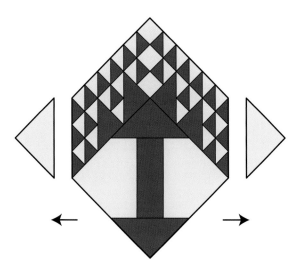

Pine Tree

Ruby Short McKim - 1928

10" Block

Patterns: pages 95-97

Cutting Instructions

Note: Some strips may have fabric left over. Measurements were figured on 40" wide fabric.

From the light fabric, cut:

1 – 5 1/4" x 14 1/2" strip – Cut the strip into 2 – 5 1/4" x 7 1/4" rectangles.

1 – 4 1/2" x 9" strip – Cut the strip into 2 – 4 1/2" squares. Cut the squares from corner to corner once on the diagonal to make triangles. 1 piece will be left over.

2 – 2 1/2" x WOF strips – Cut the strips into 18 – 2 1/2" squares. Cut the squares from corner to corner once on the diagonal to make triangles.

1 – 2 1/4" x 6 3/4" strip – Cut the strip into 3 – 2 1/4" squares.

From the dark fabric, cut:

1 – 3" square – Cut the square from corner to corner once on the diagonal to make triangles.

2 – 2 1/2" x WOF strips – Cut the strips into 21 – 2 1/2" squares. Cut the squares from corner to corner once on the diagonal to make triangles.

1 – 2 1/4" x 9" rectangle.

	Fabric	Position	Size	
Unit A – Make 1				
	Light	1	2 1/4" x 2 1/4"	
	Dark	2,4,6,8,10,12,14	2 1/2" x 2 1/2"	◻
	Light	3,5,7,9,11,13	2 1/2" x 2 1/2"	◻
Unit B – Make 1				
	Dark	1,3,5,7,9,11,13,15	2 1/2" x 2 1/2"	◻
	Light	2,4,6,8,10,12,16	2 1/2" x 2 1/2"	◻
	Light	14	2 1/4" x 2 1/4"	
Unit C – Make 1				
	Light	1,3,7,9,11,13,15,17	2 1/2" x 2 1/2"	◻
	Dark	2,4,6,8,10,12,14,16,18	2 1/2" x 2 1/2"	◻
	Light	5	2 1/4" x 2 1/4"	
Unit D – Make 1				
	Dark	1,3,5,7,9	2 1/2" x 2 1/2"	◻
	Light	2,4,6,8	2 1/2" x 2 1/2"	◻
Unit E – Make 1				
	Dark	1,3,5,7,9,11	2 1/2" x 2 1/2"	◻
	Light	2,4,6,8,10	2 1/2" x 2 1/2"	◻
Unit F – Make 1				
	Dark	1,3,5,7,9,11	2 1/2" x 2 1/2"	◻
	Light	2,4,6,8,10,12	2 1/2" x 2 1/2"	◻
	Light	13	5 1/4" x 7 1/4"	
	Dark	14	3" x 3"	◻
Unit G – Make 1				
	Light	1	5 1/4" x 7 1/4"	
	Dark	2	3" x 3"	◻
	Dark	3	2 1/4" x 9"	
	Dark	4	2 1/2" x 2 1/2"	◻
Units H, I & J – Make 1 each				
	Light	1	4 1/2" x 4 1/2"	◻

To Make the Block

1. Sew unit B to unit A.

2. Sew unit C to unit AB.

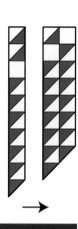

3. Sew unit D to unit E.

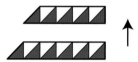

4. Sew unit F to unit G.

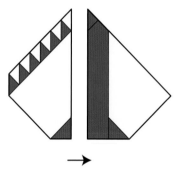

5. Sew together as shown.

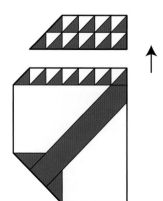

6. Sew unit H to block.

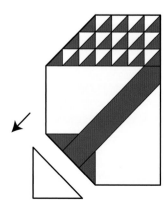

7. Sew together as shown.

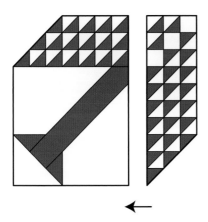

8. Sew units I and J onto each side of the block.

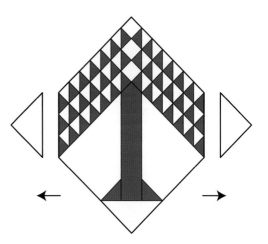

Finishing Instructions

Center Squares – Make 6

From the various light fabrics, cut:

6 – 6 1/2" squares

From the various dark fabrics, cut:

12 – 2 1/2" x 6 1/2" rectangles
12 – 2 1/2" x 10 1/2" rectangles

Sew the dark 2 1/2" x 6 1/2" rectangles to both sides of the 6 1/2" squares. Press toward the dark.

Sew the 2 1/2" x 10 1/2" rectangles to the remaining sides. Press toward the dark.

Setting Triangles – Make 10

From the various light fabrics, cut:

3 – 9 3/4" squares – Cut the squares on the diagonal twice. There will be 2 setting triangles left over.

From the various dark fabrics, cut:

10 – 2 1/2" x 9 1/4" rectangles
10 – 2 1/2" x 11 1/4" rectangles

Sew a 2 1/2" x 9 1/4" rectangle to the side of each of the setting triangles. Press toward the dark. Sew a 2 1/2" x 11 1/4" rectangle to the other side. Press toward the dark. Line up the ruler on the bottom edge and trim. Be gentle; these ends are on the bias. Make 10.

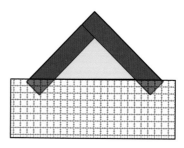

Corner Triangles – Make 4

From the various light fabrics, cut:

2 – 5 1/8" squares – Cut the squares once on the diagonal to make corner triangles.

From the various dark fabrics, cut:
4 – 2 1/2" x 12" rectangles

Center the light triangles on the dark rectangles. Sew and press toward the dark. Make 4.

Line up the ruler with the edge of the triangle as shown and trim both sides. Be gentle; these pieces also are on the bias.

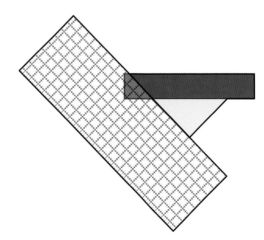

Sashing and Border
Make 58

Cutting Directions

From the various light fabrics, cut:

116 – 1 3/4" x 9 1/2" rectangles

From the red fabric, cut:

10 – 4 1/4" x WOF strips
Follow the directions below for making templates.*

3 – 11 1/2" x WOF strips. Cut the strips into 58 – 1 3/4 x 11 1/2" rectangles.

	Fabric	Position	Size
Unit A Make 58			
	Red	1	1 3/4" x 11 1/2"
	Light	2,3	1 3/4" x 9 1/2"
	Red	4,5,6,7	*Follow directions for template

*Trace template A onto template plastic or lightweight cardboard to make a template. Cut on the drawn line. Place rolled freezer tape on the back of the template to keep the template from moving. Place the template on the straight grain of fabric (see diagram on page 55) and make sure the fabric is folded with the wrong sides together so there will be a left side and a right side when cutting with the template. Reverse the template to get the optimum use of the fabric. Make sure there is at least 1/4" around the template.

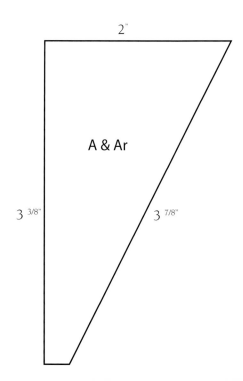

2"

A & Ar

3 3/8" 3 7/8"

Place the Add-A-Quarter with the lip side butted up to the template and cut using a rotary cutter.

Place the **bias edge** of the template A fabric along the trimmed edge of the block for units A5 and A4. Sew into place and press. Do the same for the template A reversed for units A6 and A7.

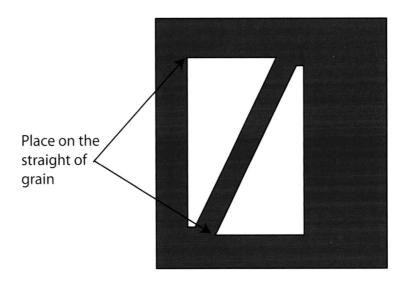

Place on the straight of grain

Cornerstones

From the various dark fabrics, cut:

17 – 3" squares

4 – 4 3/4" squares – Cut the squares on the diagonal twice. (You will have two pieces left over.)

Refer to the diagram on page page 57 and sew the center of the quilt together as shown.

First Border

From the dark fabric, cut 7 – 2 1/2" wide strips the width of the fabric.

Make 2 strips 2 1/2" x 53 1/2" and sew one to the top of the quilt and the other to the bottom of the quilt. Make 2 strips 2 1/2" x 75 1/2". Sew one to each side of the quilt.

Press the seams toward the border.

Second Border

From the red fabric, cut:

4 – 3" x 23" strips for the sides
2 – 3" x 37 1/2" strips for the top and bottom of the quilt
4 – 3" squares for the cornerstones

Refer to the diagram below and make two side borders.

Refer to the diagram below and make two borders, one for the top and one for the bottom of the quilt.

Sew the top and bottom borders in place and press toward the inside. Sew a 3" red square onto each end of the side border pieces. Sew side borders onto the quilt. Press toward the outside.

Layer quilt with backing and batting and quilt as desired.

Third Border

From the dark fabrics, cut:

8 – 6" strips the width of the fabric
Make 2 strips 6" x 62 1/2" for the top and bottom of the quilt.
Make 2 strips 6" x 91 1/2" for the sides of the quilt.

Sew a green border to the top and bottom. Press toward the outside. Sew green side borders onto the quilt. Refer to the diagram on page 57.

Layer quilt with backing and batting and quilt as desired.

Binding
From the red fabric, cut:

9 – 2 1/4" strips the width of the fabric

Black Forest

Made by Carolyn Cullinan McCormick
Quilted by Susan Bateman, Parker, Colorado

Trees, Trees and More Trees

Made by Carolyn Cullinan McCormick
Quilted by Bonnie Colonna, Castle Rock, Colorado

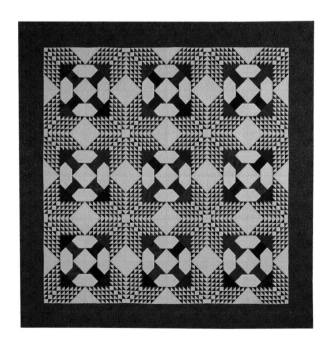

Can't See the Trees for the Forest

Made by Carolyn Cullinan McCormick
Quilted by Carol Willey, Castle Rock, Colorado

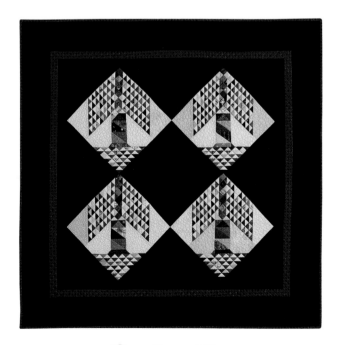

Confetti Trees

Made by Carolyn Cullinan McCormick
Quilted by Susan Bateman, Parker, Colorado

Fall in the Rockies

Made by Megan McCormick, Parker, Colorado, Carol Netwal, Castle Rock, Colorado, Diane Donnelly, Bozeman, Montana, Carol Bonetti, Castle Rock, Colorado, Marilyn Vap, Castle Rock, Colorado, Bonnie Colonna, Castle Rock, Colorado, Jan Korytkowski, Castle Rock, Colorado, Ginny Rafferty, Castle Rock, Colorado, Connie Stewart, Castle Rock, Colorado, Nancy Plekan, Parker, Colorado, Wendy Kay, Castle Rock, Colorado and Marie Llanes, Denver, Colorado. Quilted by Susan Bateman, Parker, Colorado.

Tennessee Trees

Made by Carolyn Cullinan McCormick
Quilted by Bonnie Colonna, Castle Rock, Colorado

Patterns

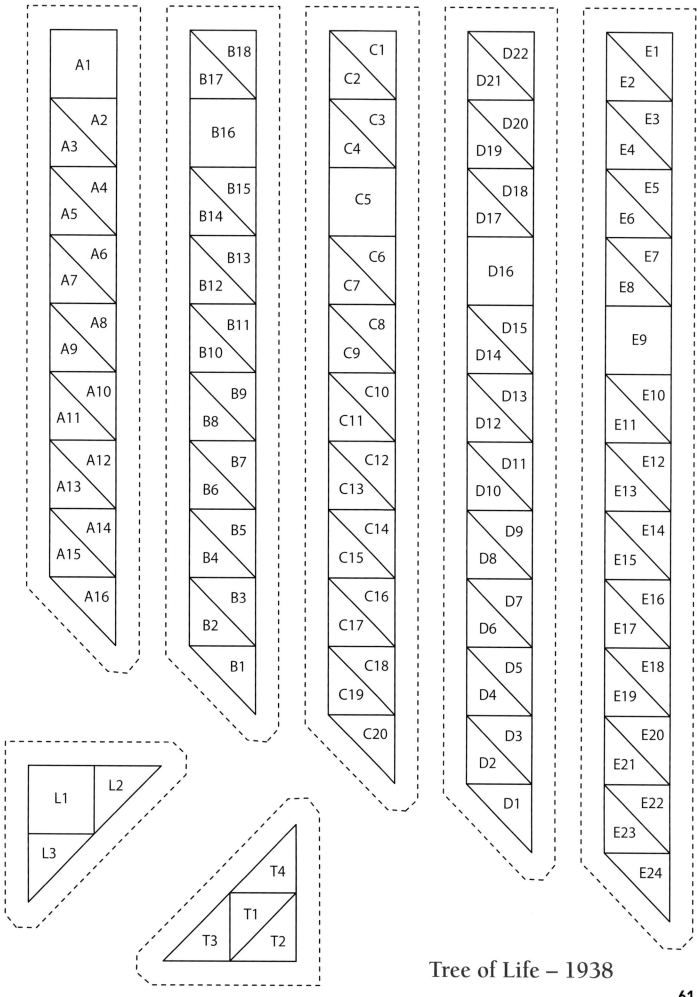

Tree of Life – 1938

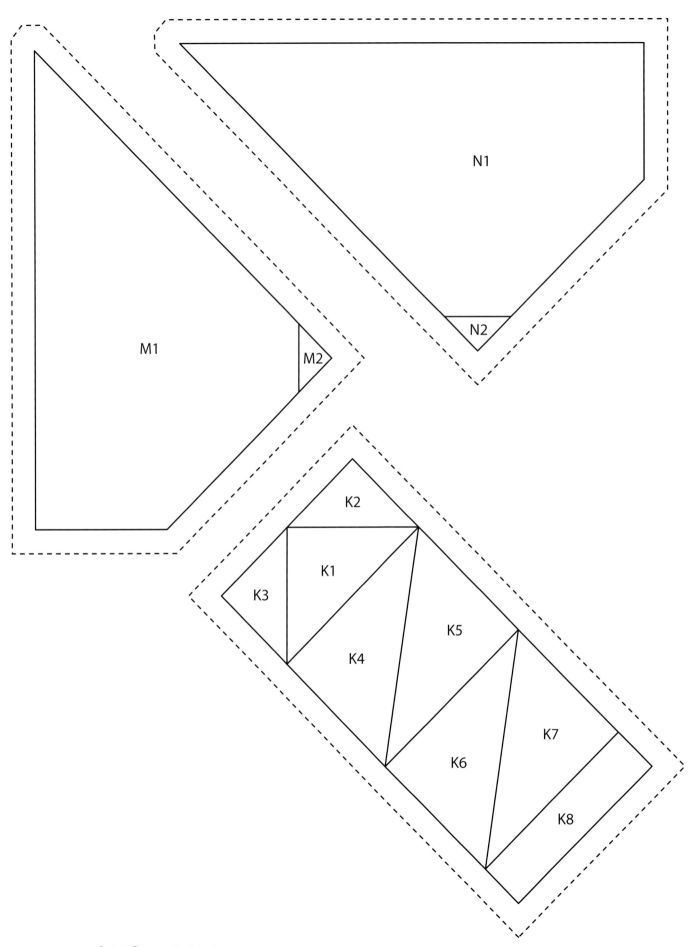

Tree of Life – 1938

Tree of Life – 1938

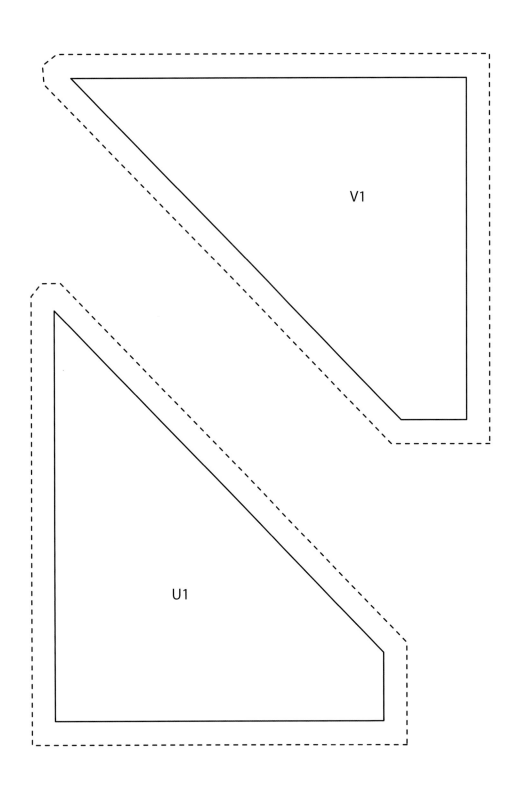

V1

U1

Tree of Life – 1938

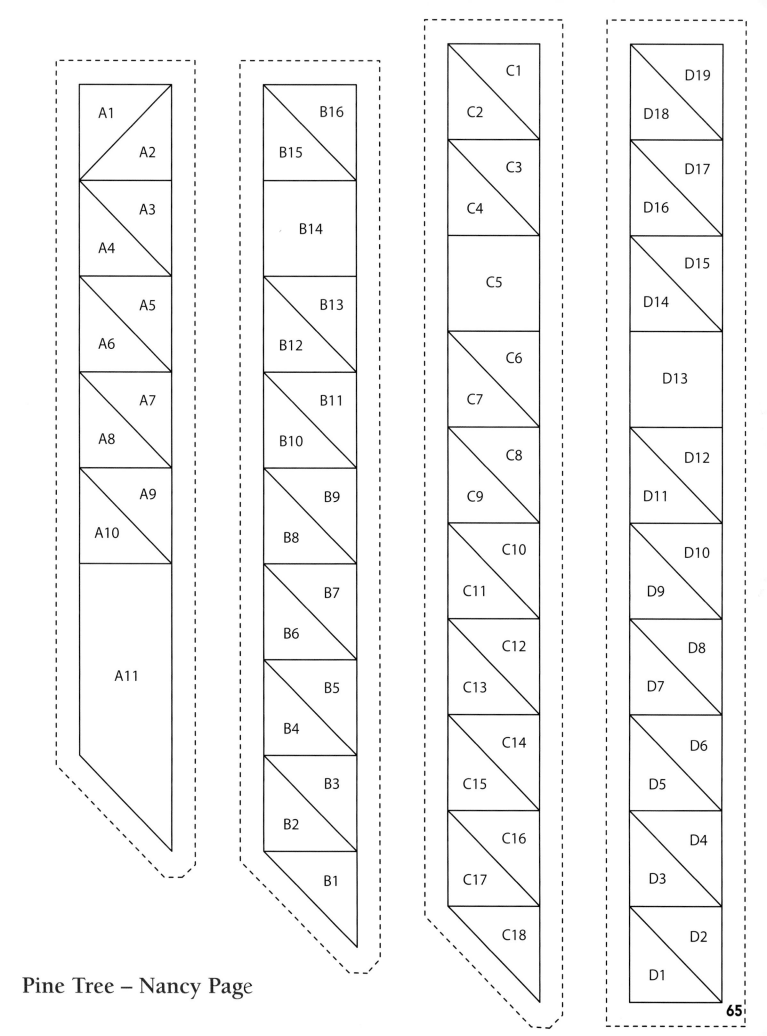

Pine Tree – Nancy Page

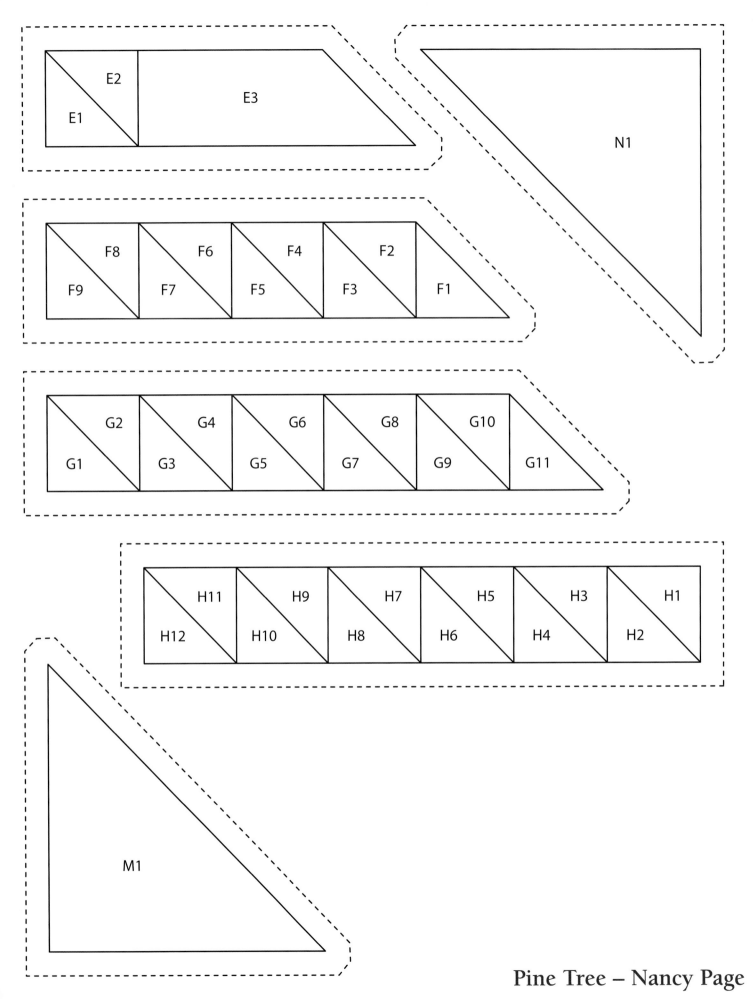

Pine Tree – Nancy Page

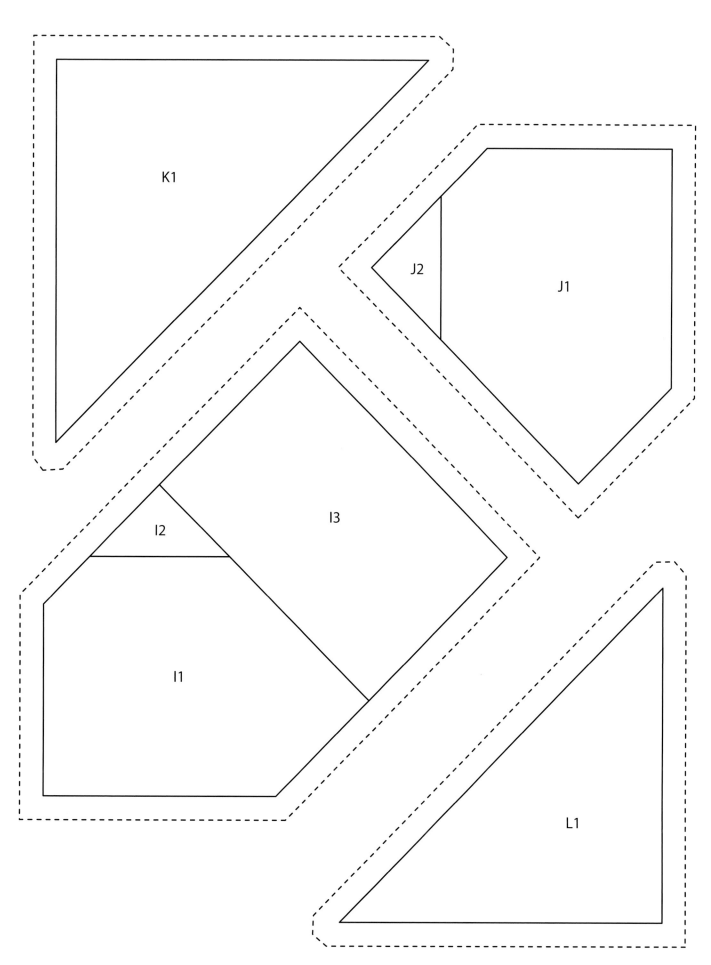

Pine Tree – Nancy Page

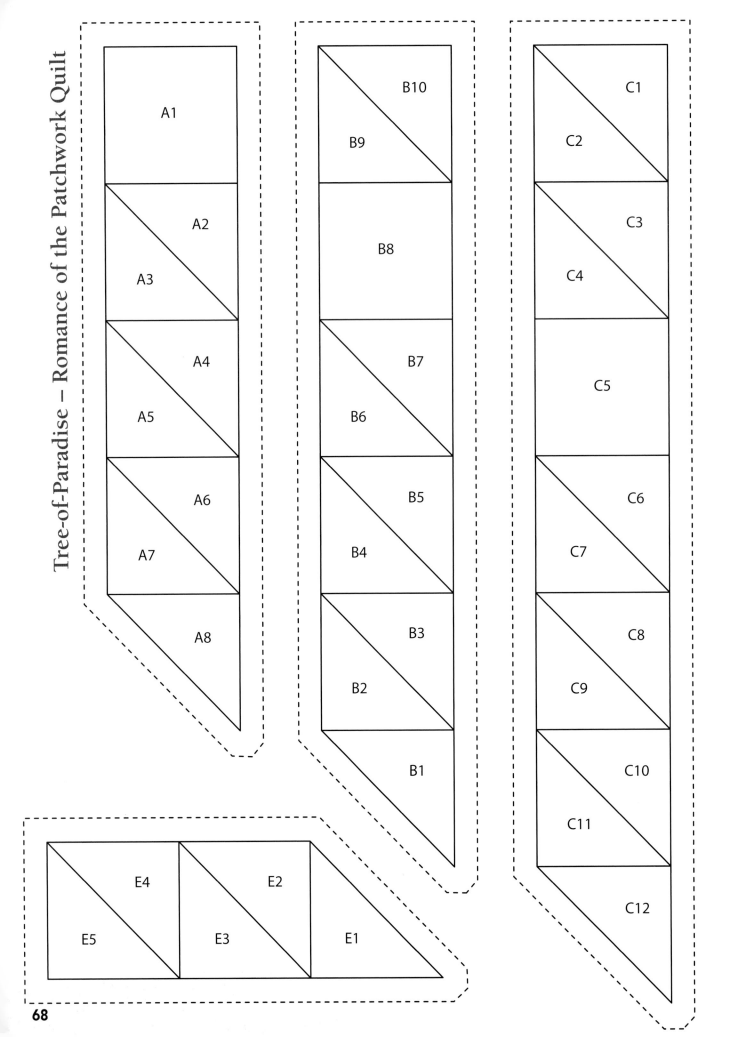

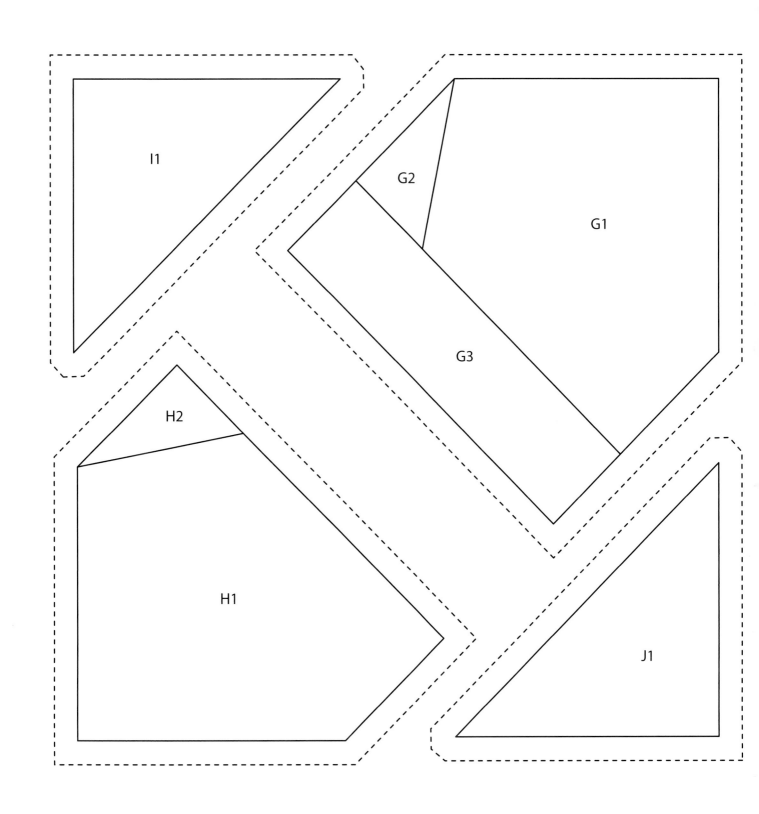

Tree-of-Paradise – Romance of the Patchwork Quilt

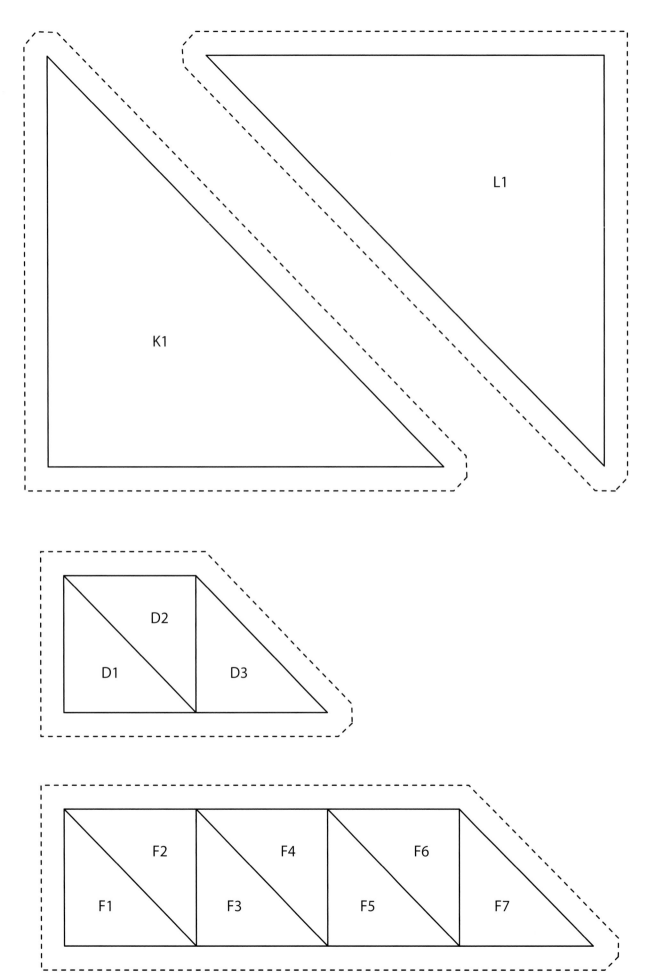

K1

L1

D2

D1

D3

F2

F4

F6

F1

F3

F5

F7

Tree-of-Paradise – Romance of the Patchwork Quilt

Tree of Paradise

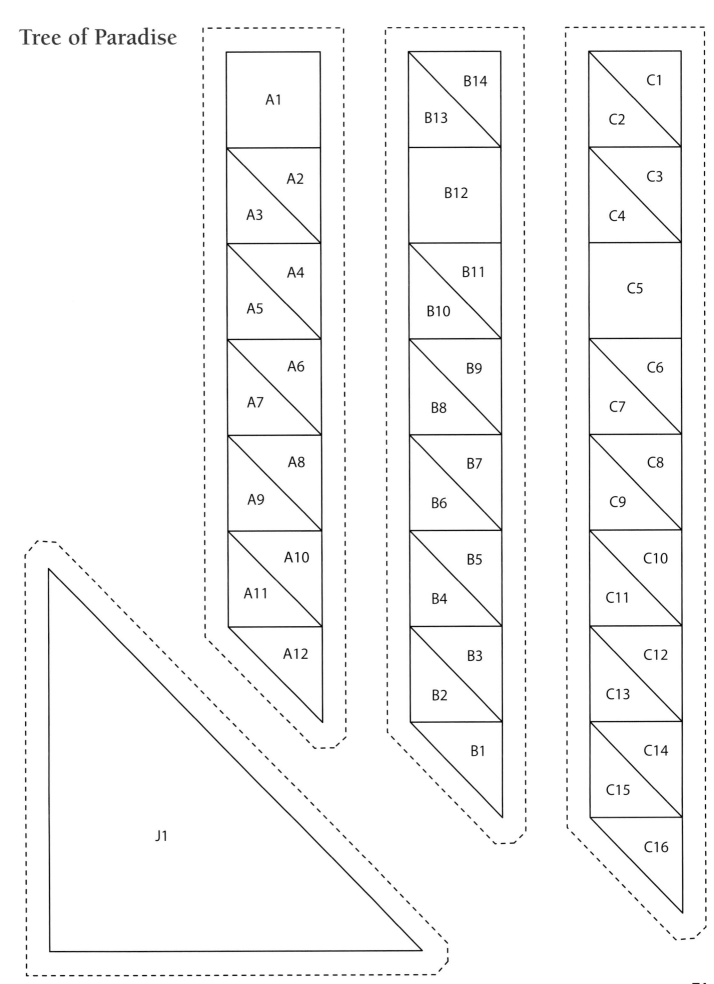

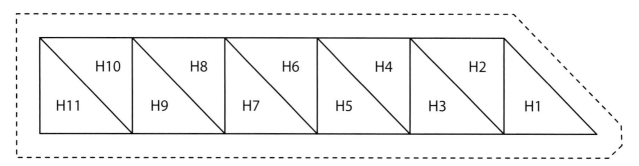

Tree of Paradise

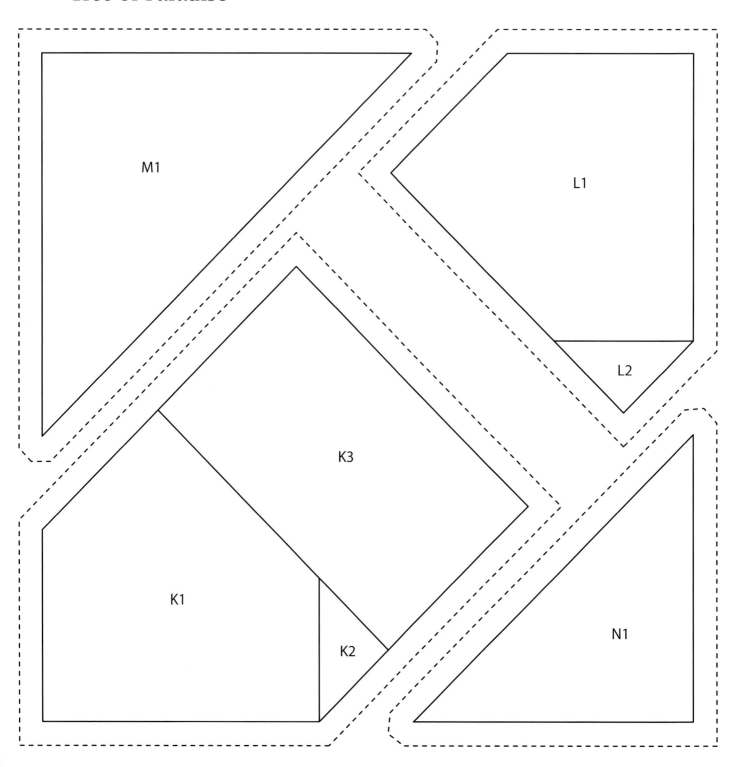

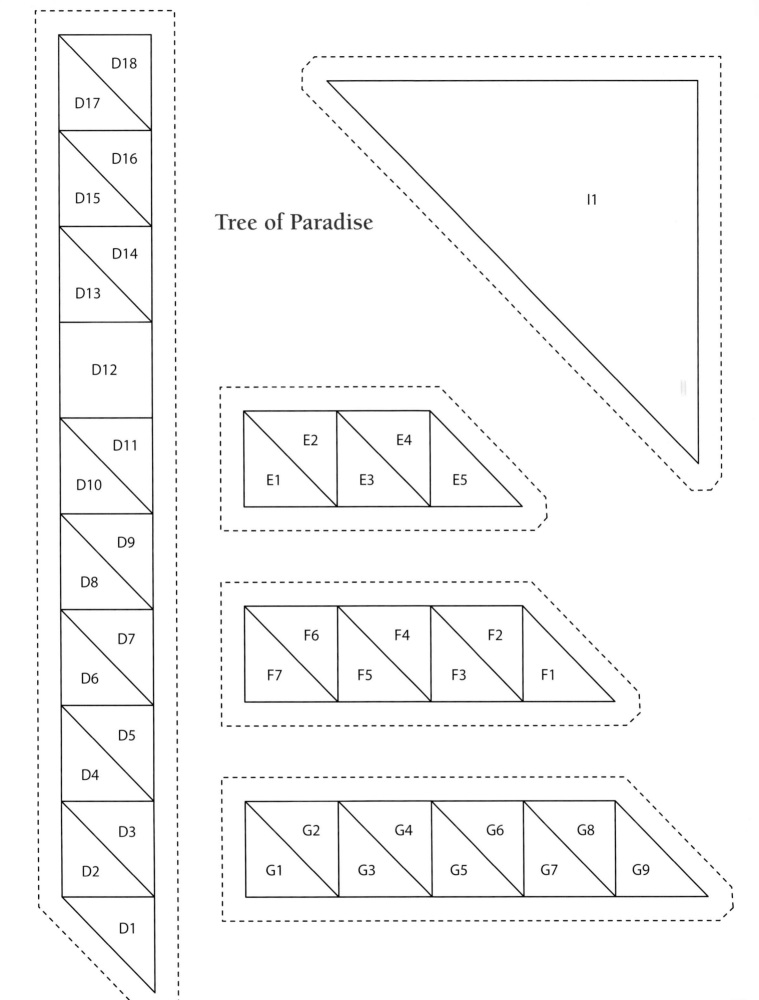

Tree of Paradise

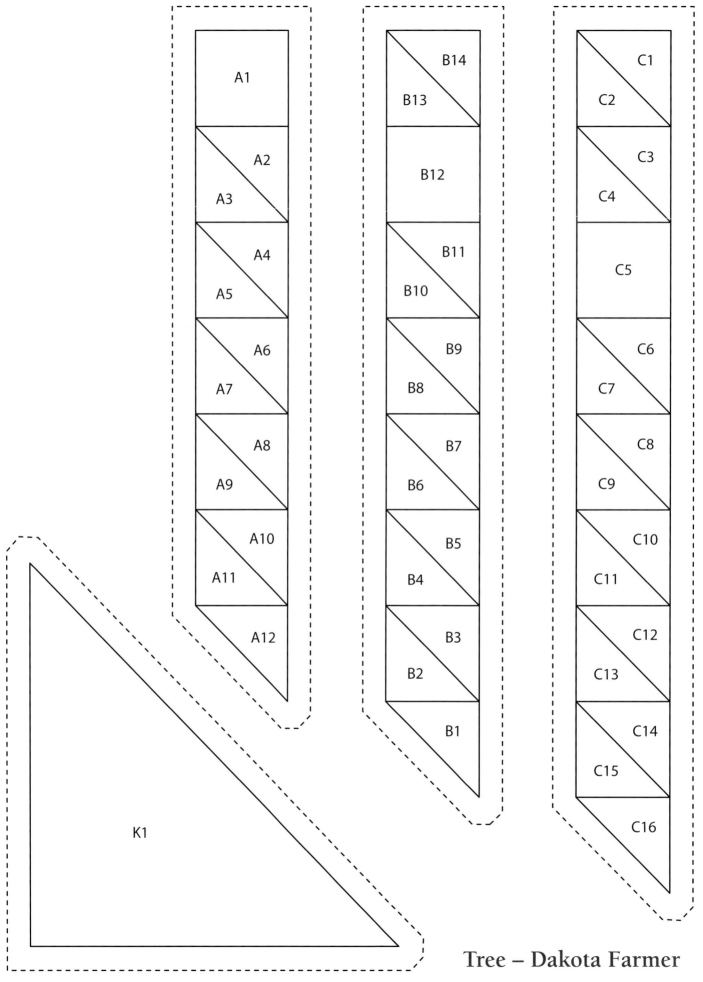

Tree – Dakota Farmer

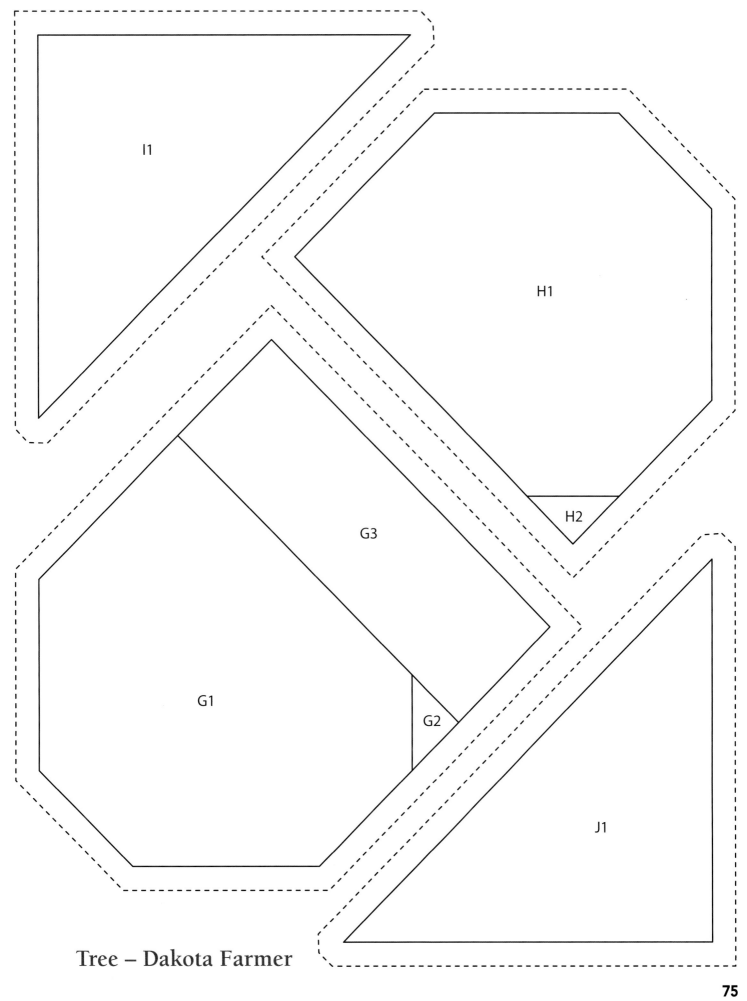

I1

H1

H2

G3

G1

G2

J1

Tree – Dakota Farmer

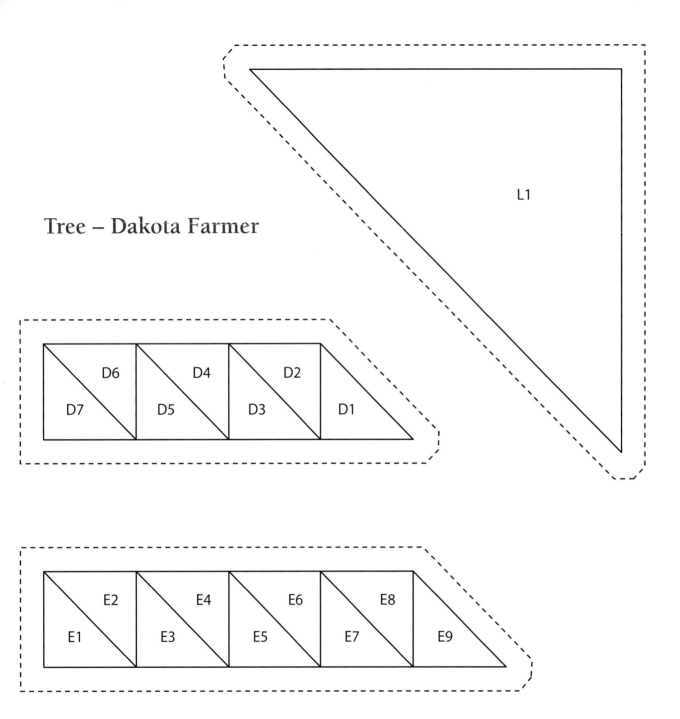

Tree – Dakota Farmer

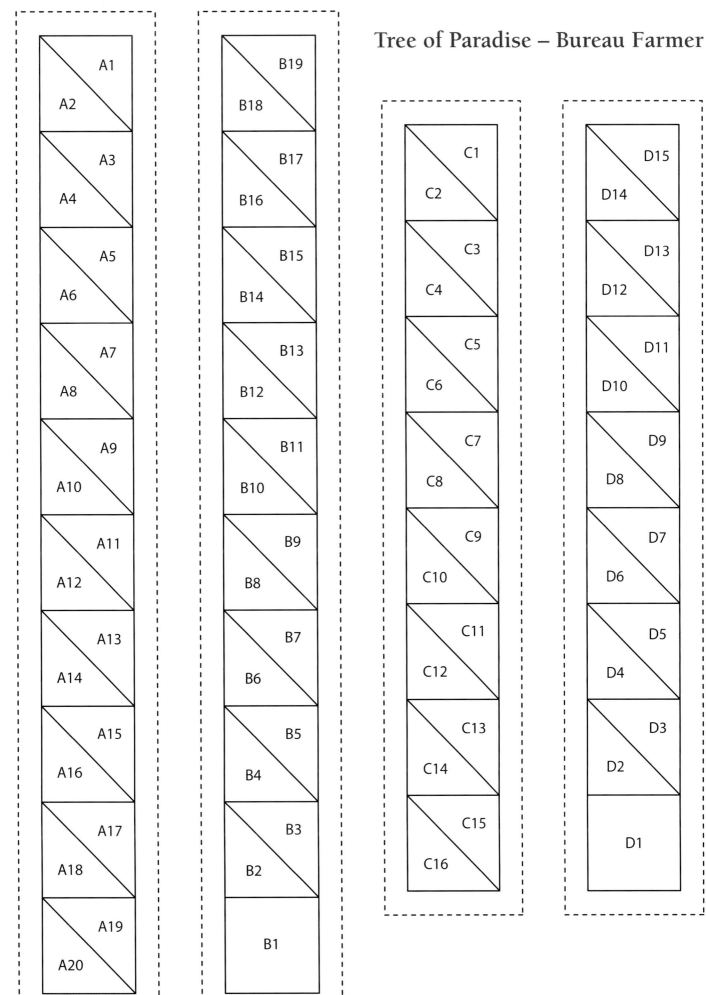

Tree of Paradise – Bureau Farmer

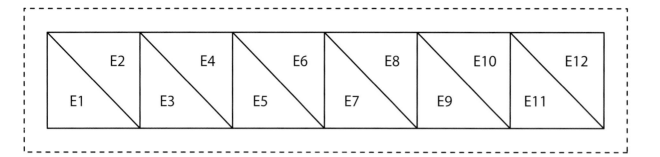

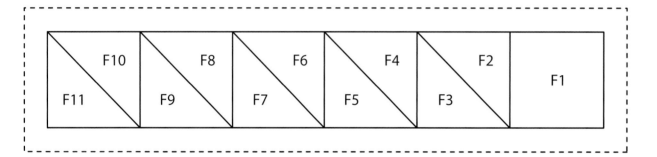

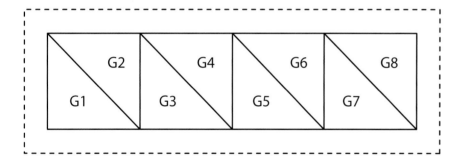

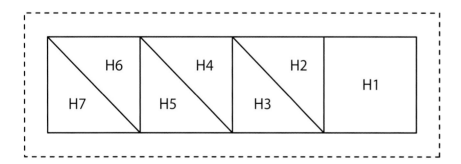

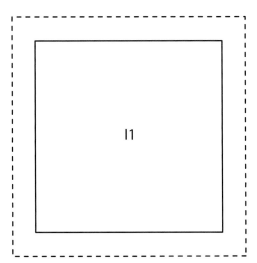

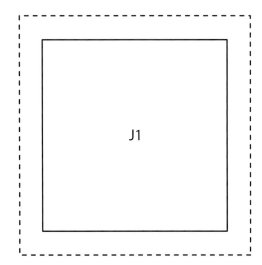

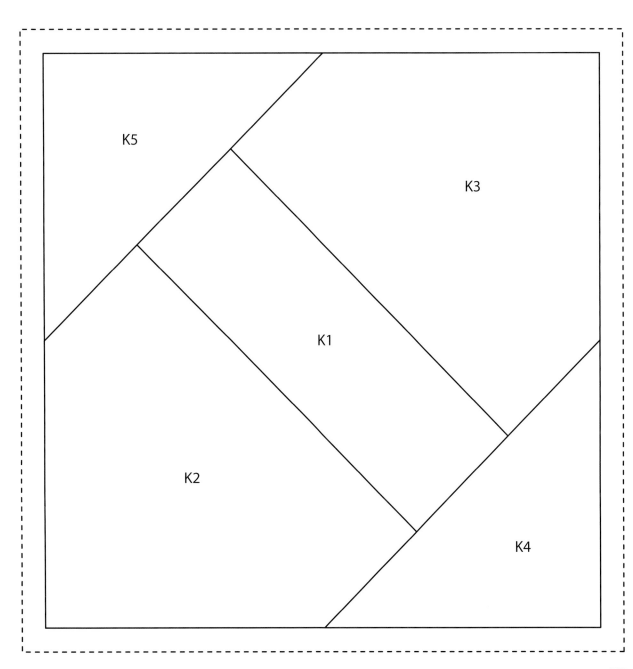

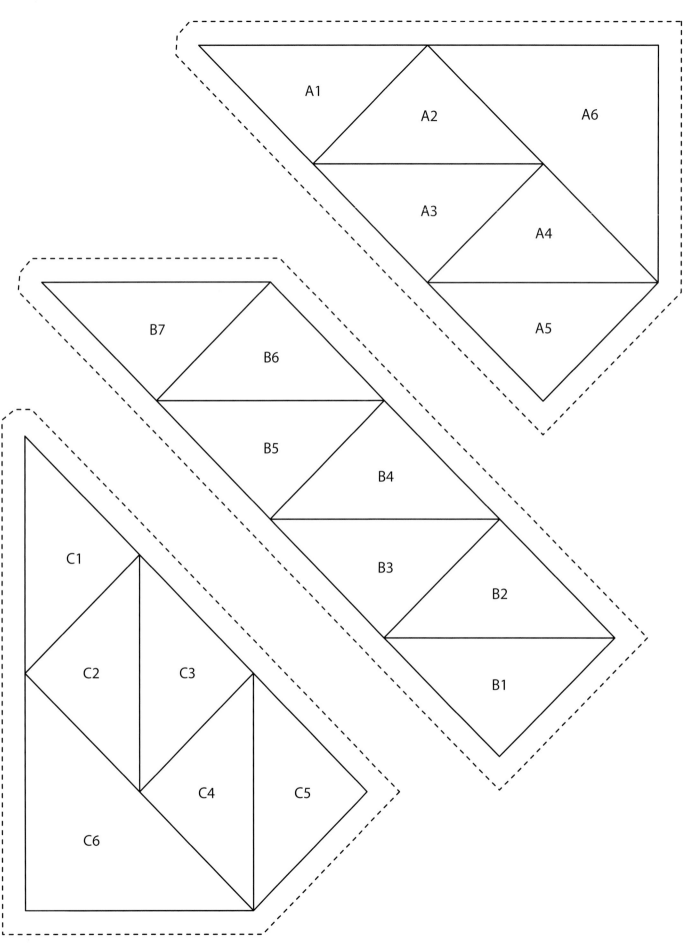

Tennessee Pine

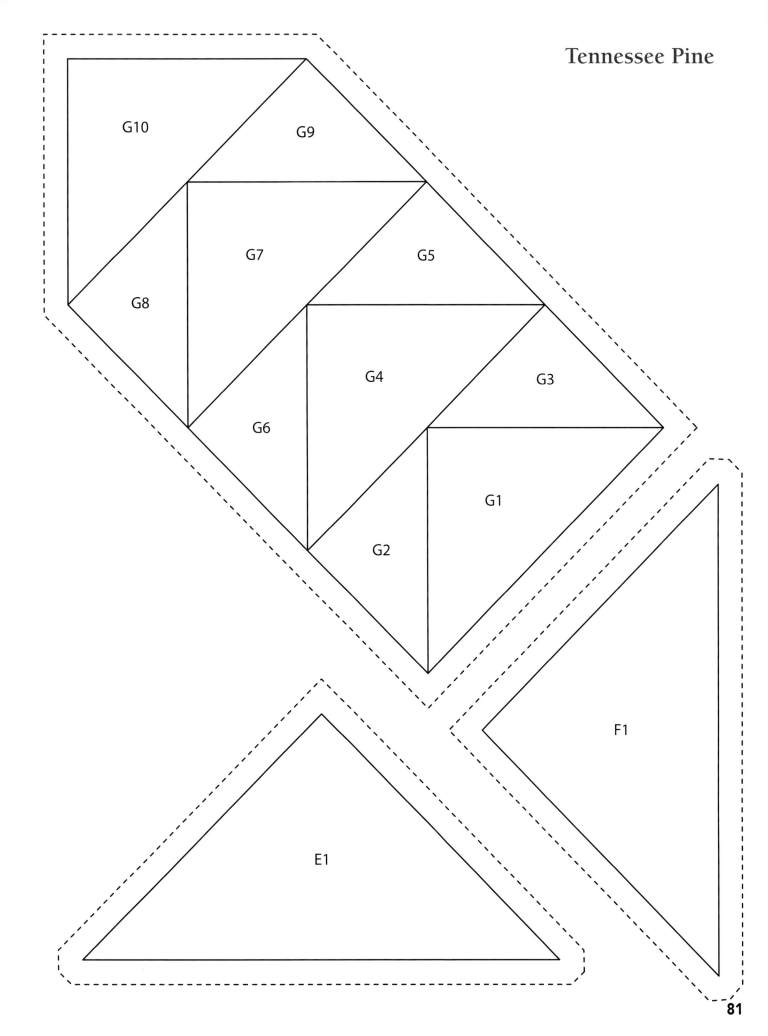

Tennessee Pine

G10

G9

G7

G5

G8

G4

G3

G6

G1

G2

F1

E1

Tennessee Pine

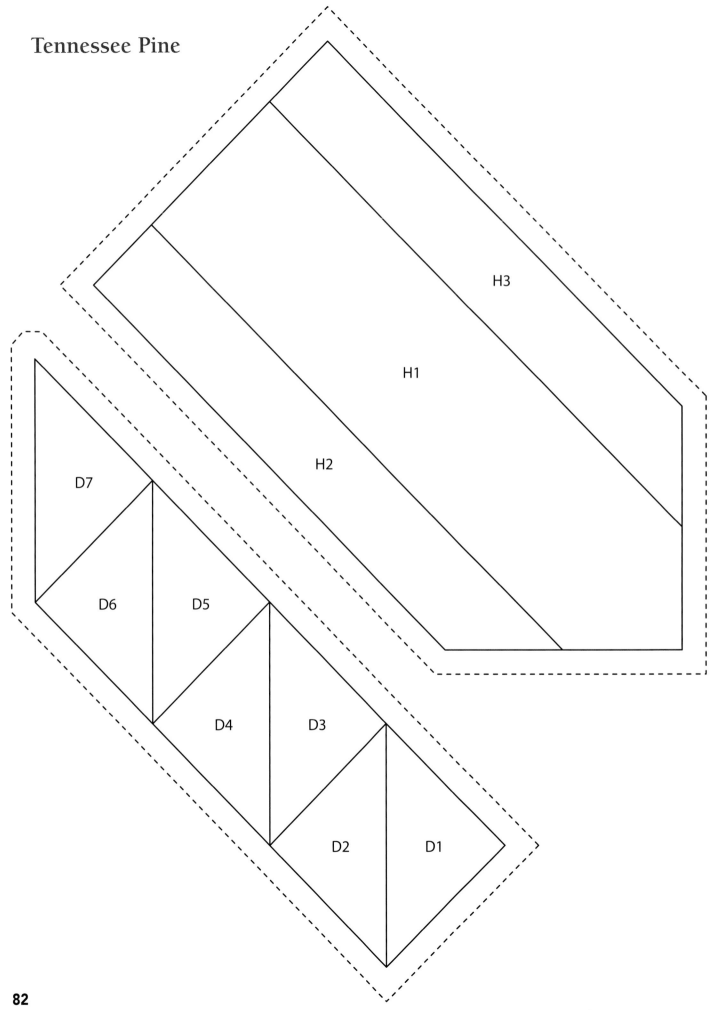

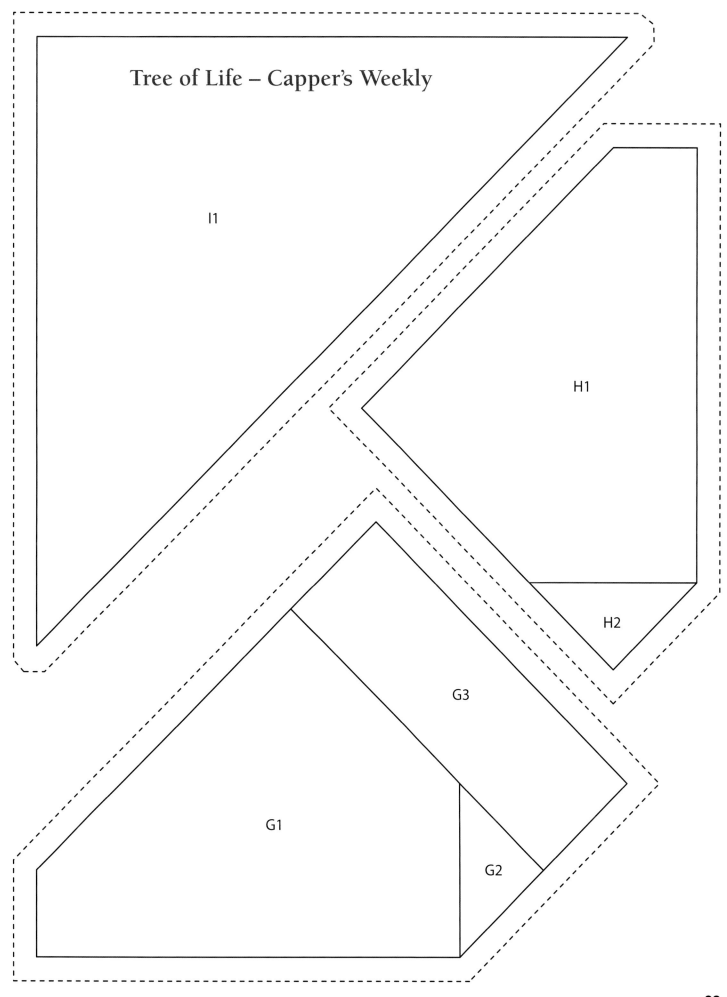

Tree of Life – Capper's Weekly

I1

H1

H2

G3

G1

G2

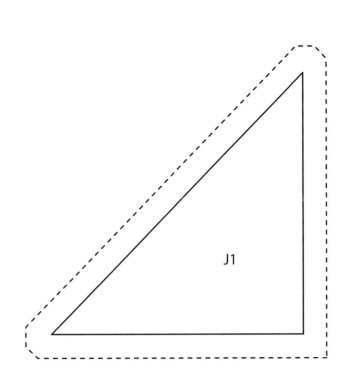

J1

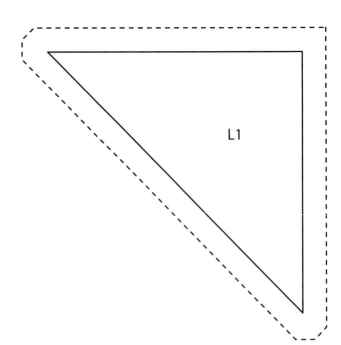

L1

Tree of Life – Capper's Weekly

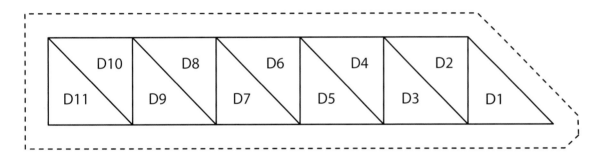

| | D10 | | D8 | | D6 | | D4 | | D2 | |
| D11 | | D9 | | D7 | | D5 | | D3 | | D1 |

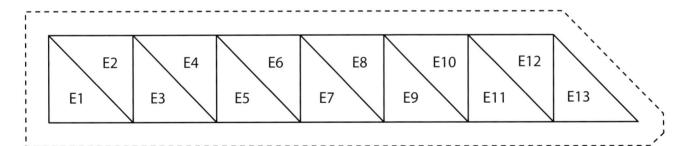

| E2 | | E4 | | E6 | | E8 | | E10 | | E12 | |
| E1 | | E3 | | E5 | | E7 | | E9 | | E11 | | E13 |

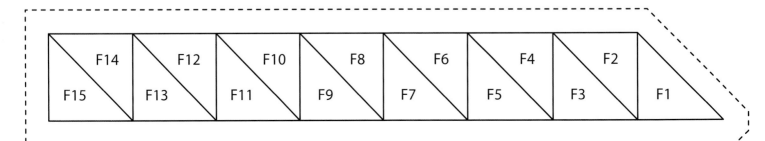

| | F14 | | F12 | | F10 | | F8 | | F6 | | F4 | | F2 | |
| F15 | | F13 | | F11 | | F9 | | F7 | | F5 | | F3 | | F1 |

Tree of Life – Capper's Weekly

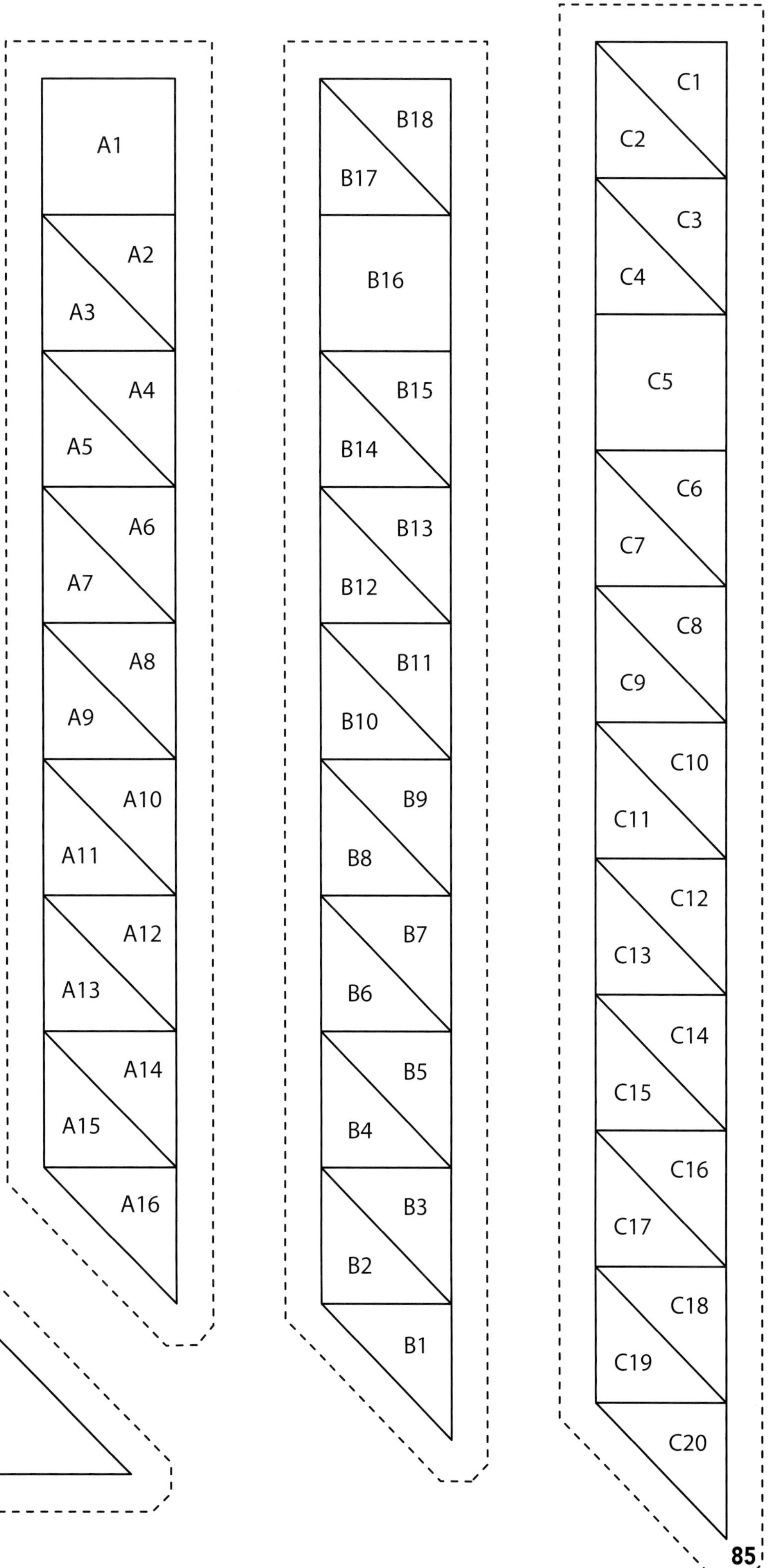

A1

A2
A3

A4
A5

A6
A7

A8
A9

A10
A11

A12
A13

A14
A15

A16

B18
B17

B16

B15
B14

B13

B12

B11

B10

B9

B8

B7

B6

B5

B4

B3

B2

B1

C1
C2

C3
C4

C5

C6
C7

C8
C9

C10
C11

C12
C13

C14
C15

C16
C17

C18
C19

C20

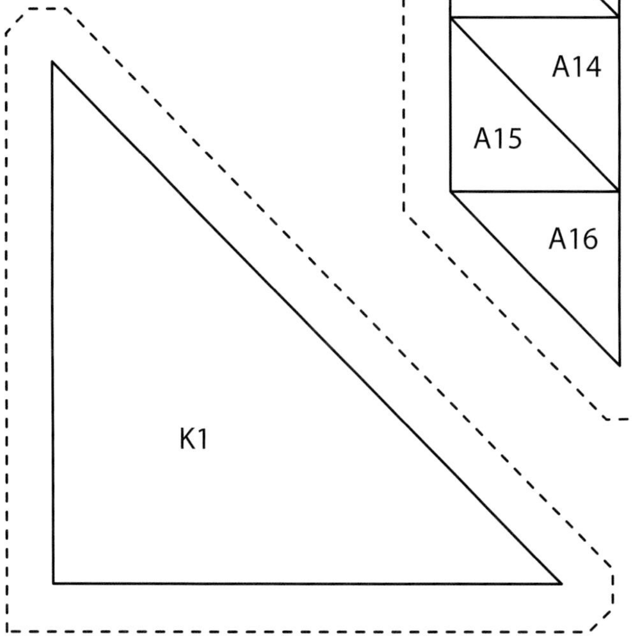

K1

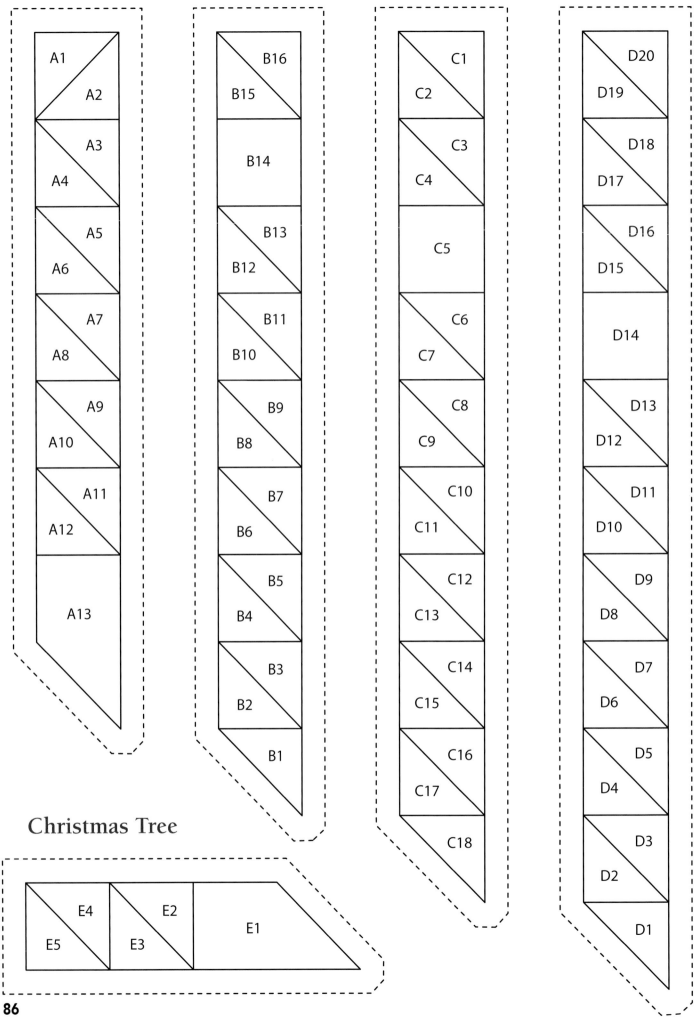

Christmas Tree

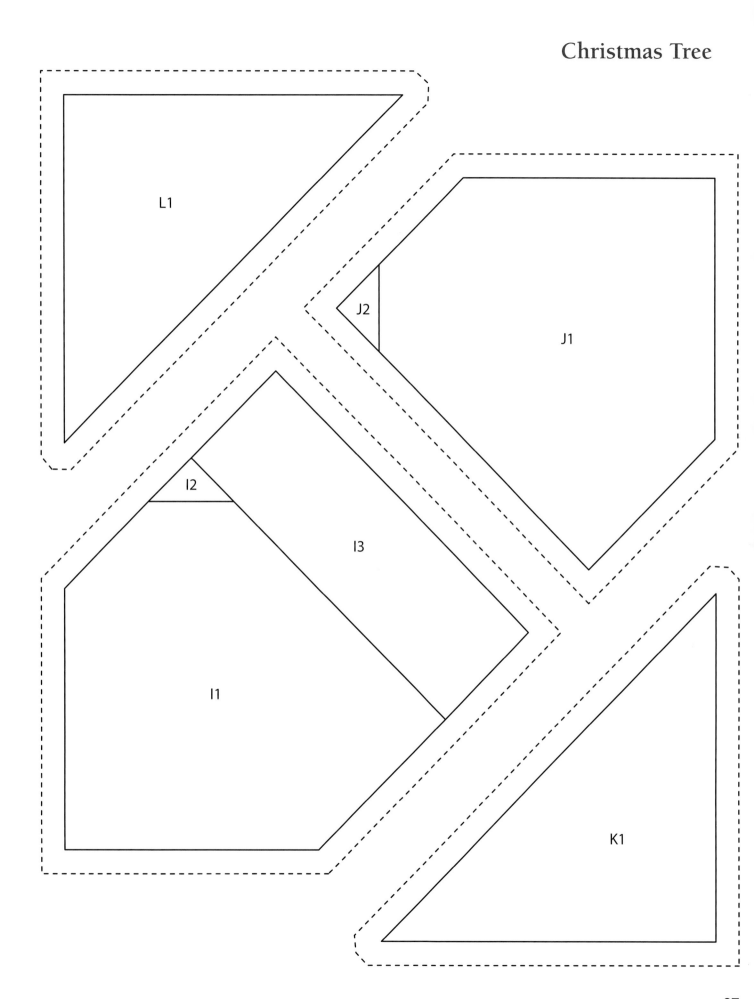

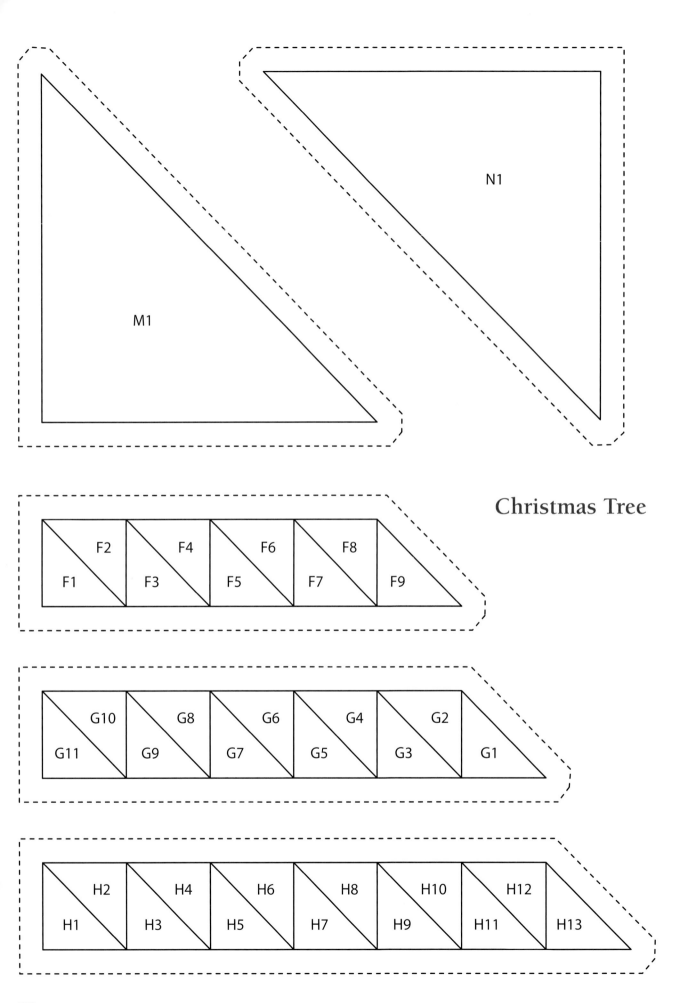

Christmas Tree

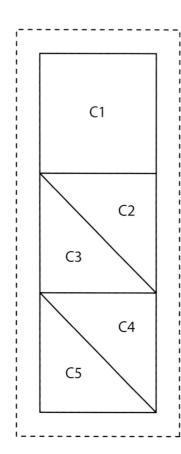

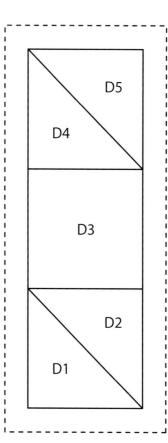

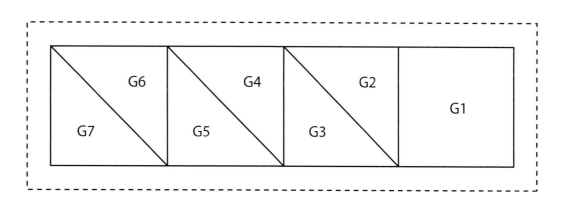

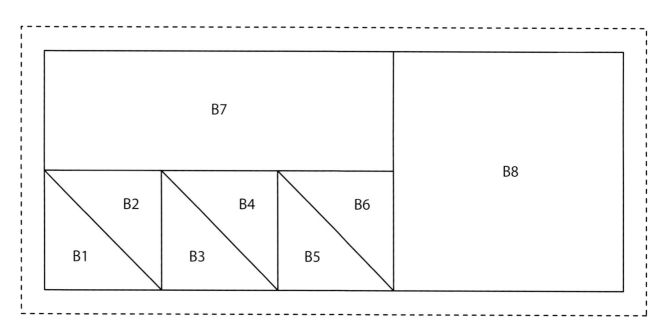

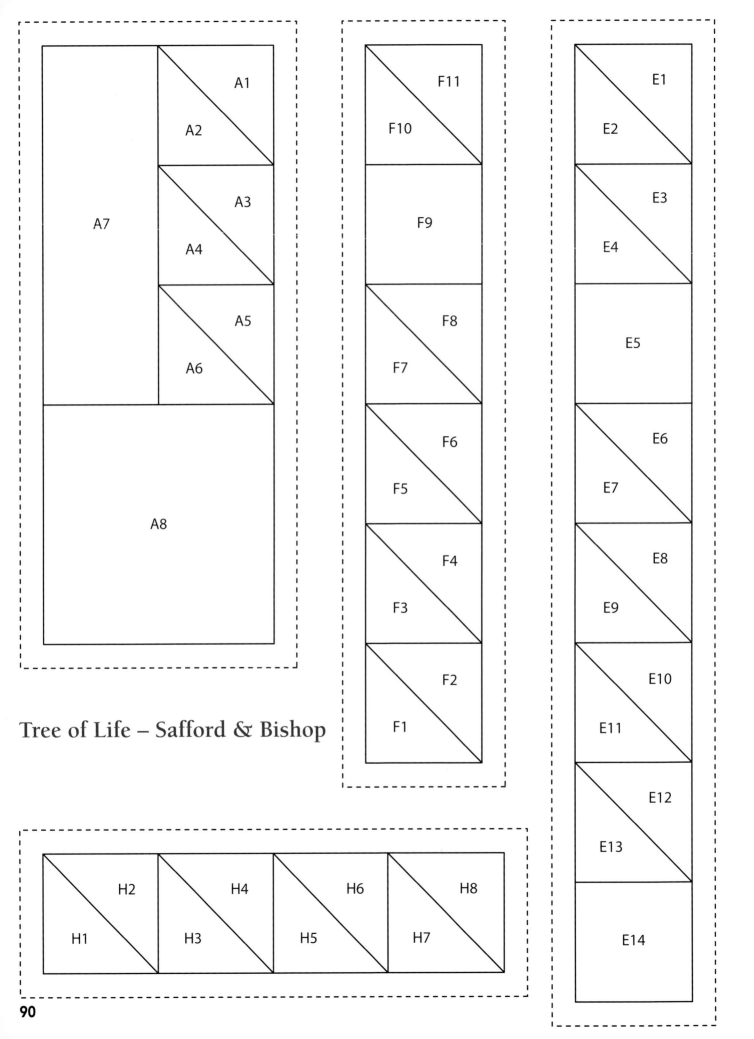

Tree of Life – Safford & Bishop

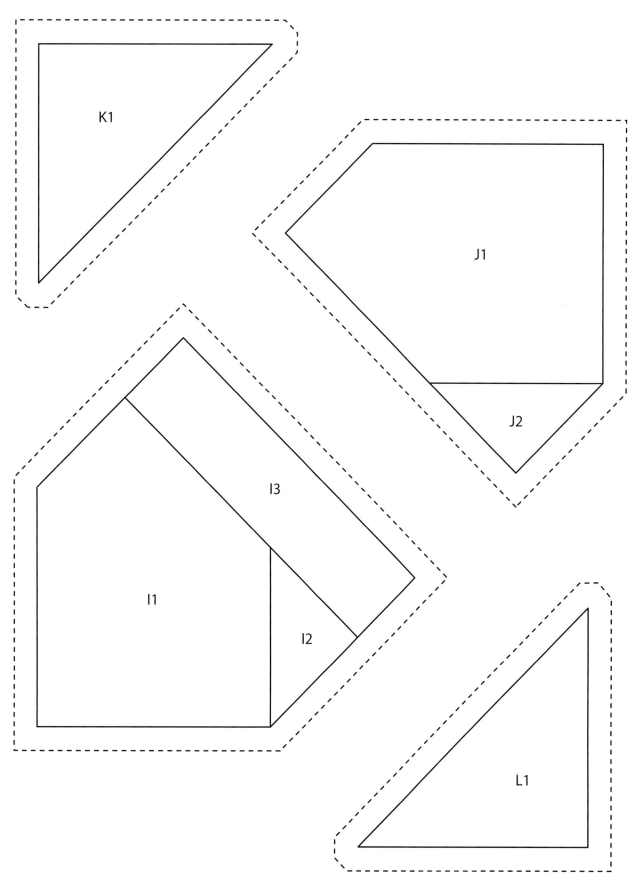

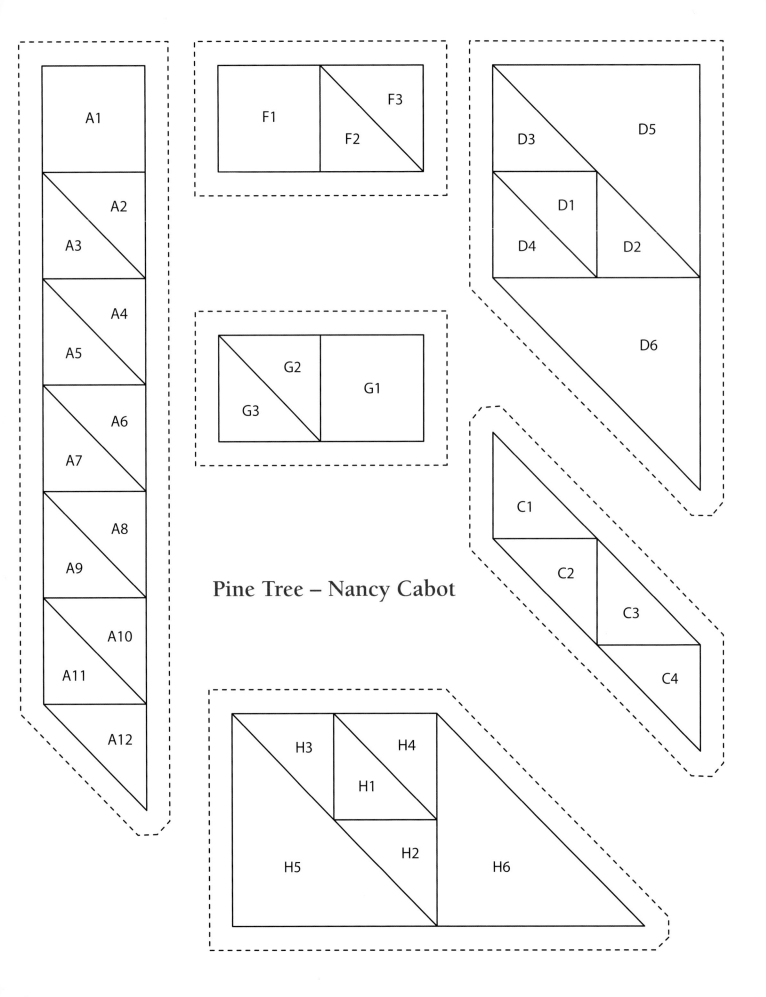

Pine Tree – Nancy Cabot

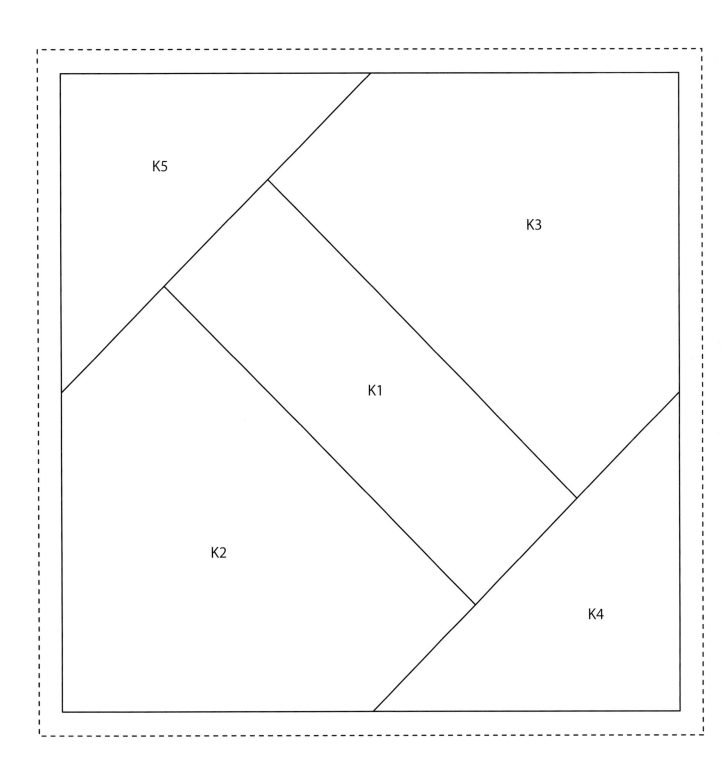

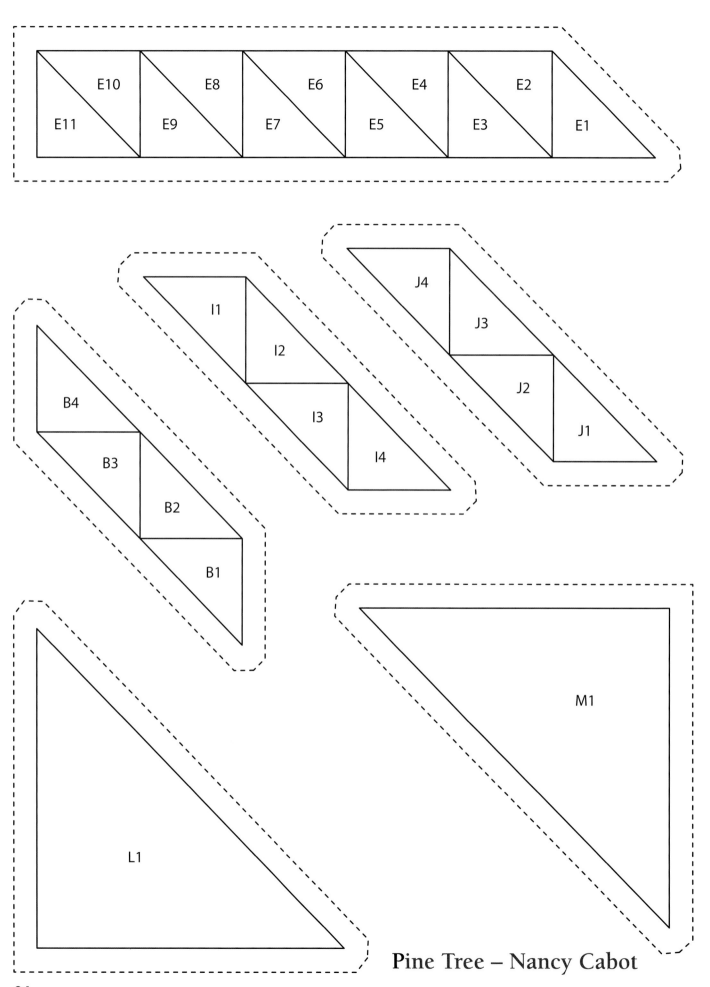

Pine Tree – Nancy Cabot

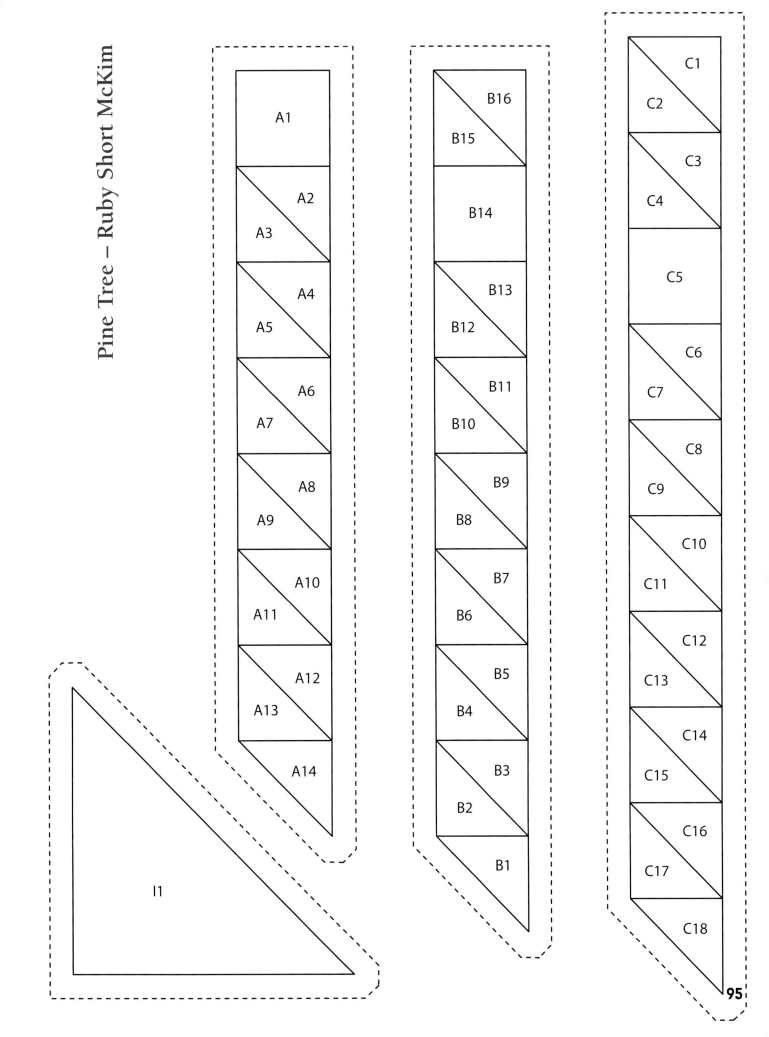

Pine Tree – Ruby Short McKim

A1
A2
A3
A4
A5
A6
A7
A8
A9
A10
A11
A12
A13
A14

I1

B16
B15
B14
B13
B12
B11
B10
B9
B8
B7
B6
B5
B4
B3
B2
B1

C1
C2
C3
C4
C5
C6
C7
C8
C9
C10
C11
C12
C13
C14
C15
C16
C17
C18

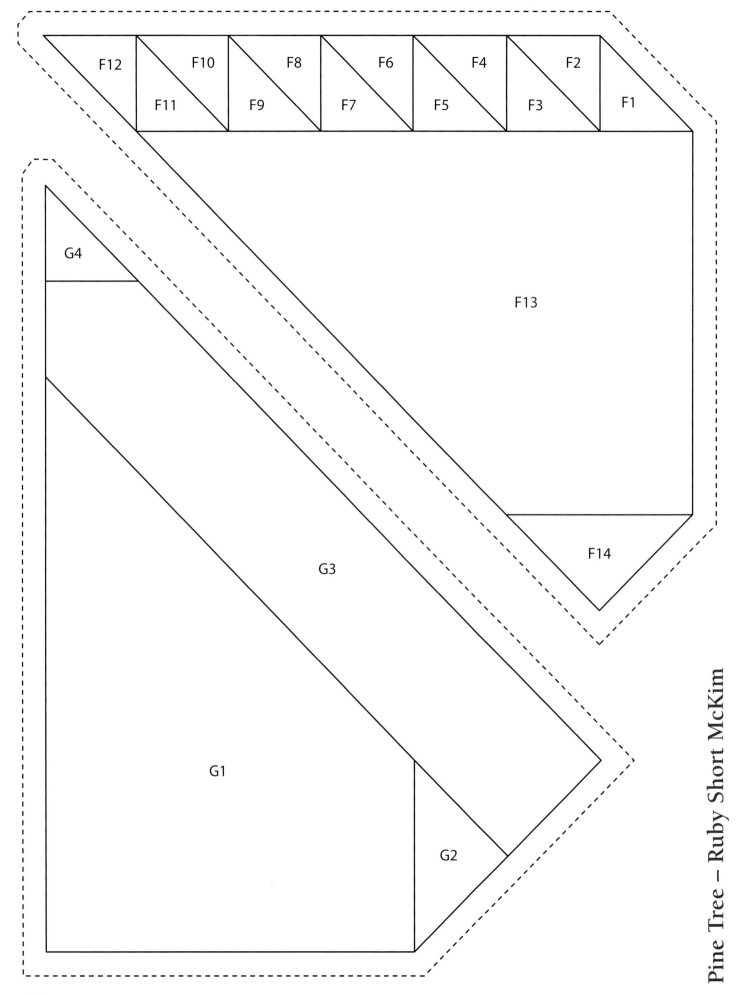

Pine Tree – Ruby Short McKim

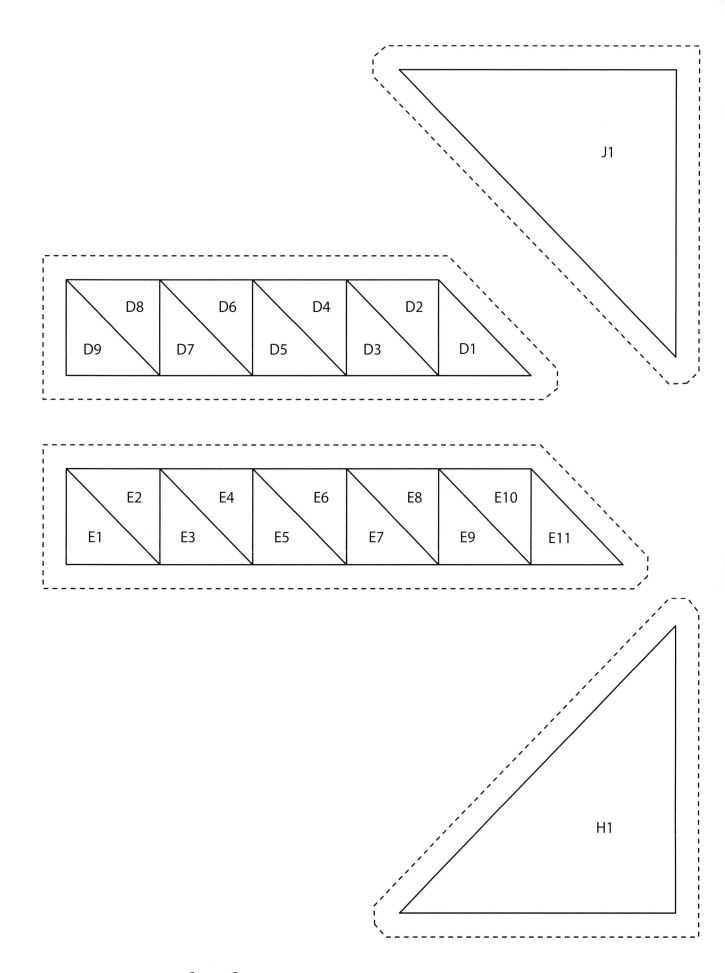

Pine Tree – Ruby Short McKim

Resources

Add-A-Quarter®
CM Designs, Inc
7968 Kelty Trail
Franktown, Colo. 80116
Phone: 303-841-5920
Web: www.addaquarter.com
E-mail: addaqtr@msn.com

Fabric

Robert Kaufman Fabrics
129 W. 132nd St.
Los Angeles, Cal. 90061
Phone: 800-877-2066
Web: www.robertkaufman.com

Moda Fabrics
13800 Hutton Dr.
Dallas, Texas 75234
Phone: 972-484-8901
Web: www.modafabrics.com

Batting

The Warm Company
5529 -186th Place SW
Lynnwood, Wash. 98037
Phone: 425-248-2424
Web: www.warmcompany.com

Long-arm Quilters

Willey Nice Quilts
Carol Willey
Castle Rock, Colo.
Phone: 303-517-4000
E-mail: WilleyNiceQuilts@live.com

Susan Bateman
Parker, Colo.

Quilted Collectibles
Bonnie Colonna
Castle Rock, Colo.
Phone: 303-722-0650
E-mail: bcolonna33@msn.com

How To Paper Piece

Why paper piece?

Paper piecing is great for beginners as well as experienced quilters. One can make a wonderful quilt on their very first try since complicated patterns are broken down into easily managed steps. Sewing the fabric to paper makes matching points relatively easy and the paper stabilizes the fabric, enabling one to use even the smallest of scraps.

Get Ready …

1. Use a copy machine to copy your pattern. Make all of your copies from the same original and use the same copy machine. All copy machines distort to some extent so check your pattern by holding the original and the copy together with a light source behind the two sheets of paper. Make as many copies as necessary. It's nice to have a few extras in case you make an error. Use the lightest weight paper you can find. The heavier the paper, the more difficult it is to remove.

2. Use a 90/14-size needle and set the stitch length to 18-20 stitches per inch. The larger needle perforates the paper making it easier to tear off. The small stitches keep the seams from ripping out when you remove the paper.

3. Place a piece of muslin or scrap fabric on your ironing board. When you press the pieces, the ink from the copies can transfer onto your ironing board cover. **Caution:** Please be aware that the dye in dye-based inks in ink-jet printers will dissolve when exposed to water, thus there is a possibility for the ink to transfer onto your fabric when using steam for pressing. Pigmented inks are more water resistant than dye-based inks. Please check to make sure that your ink does not dissolve when exposed to water/steam.

4. Have a light source nearby. The light on your sewing machine is usually adequate.

5. Remember: when paper piecing your pattern will be reversed.

Get Set …

(see Fig.A – Fig. L on page 100)

1. Here is a familiar pattern **(see Fig. A).** Instead of templates with seam allowances, as many of us are used to seeing, paper-piecing patterns have lines and numbers. The numbers indicate the sequence in which to sew. The only seam allowances that are shown are the ones that go around either the block or the unit.

2. The front of the pattern is where the lines and numbers are printed. This is the side you will sew on. The back of the pattern is the side that is blank. This is where your fabric will be placed.

3. Cut your fabric pieces according to the cutting chart for each block. Always make sure the pieces of fabric are at least 1/4" larger all the way around than shown on the foundation paper.

Sew!

1. Put fabric number 1 **RIGHT SIDE UP** on the blank side of the pattern. Use a pin or double-sided tape to hold the piece in place. The tape allows the fabric to lie flat on the paper. The pin can make a small rise in the paper **(see Fig. B).**

2. Turn the foundation pattern over. Hold the paper in front of your light source and make sure the fabric extends beyond the lines on all sides by at least 1/4" **(see Fig. C).**

3. Place an index card or template plastic on the sewing line between piece number 1 and piece number 2. Fold the foundation pattern back over the edge of the card. You can now see the excess fabric from piece number 1 **(see Fig. D).**

4. Place the Add-A-Quarter ruler up against the fold of the foundation paper with the lip side down and against the fold. Use a rotary cutter to trim the extra fabric from piece number 1 to exactly 1/4". You will now have a straight edge for placing fabric piece number 2 **(see Fig. E).**

5. Place the fabric that goes in position number 2 along the trimmed edge of piece number 1, right sides facing **(see Fig. F).**

6. Turn the foundation paper over and stitch on the line between piece number 1 and piece number 2. Sew a few stitches before the line begins and a few stitches after the line ends. Make sure piece number 2 does not slip **(see Fig. G).**

7. Open piece number 2 and press using a dry iron **(see Fig. H).**

8. Fold the foundation paper back along the line between piece number 1 and piece number 3 using the index card or template plastic. Butt the Add-A-Quarter ruler up against the fold and trim the excess fabric **(see Fig. I).**

9. Turn the foundation back over and position fabric piece number 3, being careful not to displace your fabric. Sew on the line between number 1 and number 3 **(see Fig. J and K).**

10. Continue sewing each piece in place in the numeric order given until each unit is complete **(see Fig. L).**

11. After all the pieces are sewn onto the foundation trim the edges on the outside (dotted) lines. **NEVER TRIM ON THE SOLID LINE!** Line your ruler up along the dotted line and trim the seam allowance with a rotary cutter.

12. If you are paper piecing a block that is made up of multiple units, the time has come to sew them together. Pin the units together. Make sure the lines match up on the top and bottom by putting a pin straight through both lines at each intersection. Check to make sure the seam lines also line up, or your block will be off.

13. DO NOT REMOVE THE PAPER YET. It is best to join the bocks before removing the paper, thus giving you a line to follow when you join the blocks.

14. After all of the blocks are sewn together it is time to remove the paper. A pair of tweezers can be helpful for removing small pieces and corners.

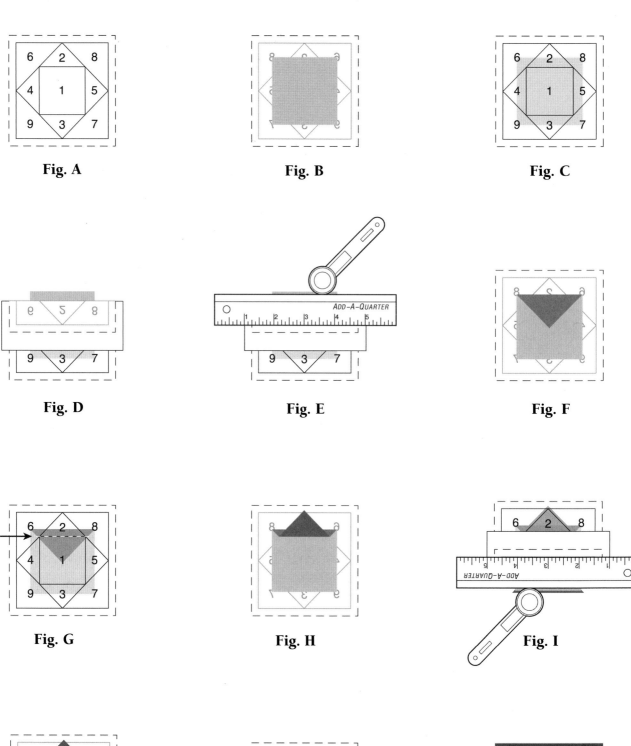

Fig. A

Fig. B

Fig. C

Fig. D

Fig. E

Fig. F

Stitch here

Fig. G

Fig. H

ADD-A-QUARTER

Fig. I

Fig. J

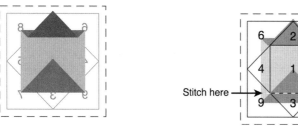

Stitch here

Fig. K

Fig. L